Lois Lowry

by Lois Markham

The Learning Works, Inc.
Santa Barbara, California

The
Learning
Works

Edited by
Jan Stiles

Page Design and Editorial Production by
Clark Editorial & Design

Cover Photo by
Bachrach

To my mother,
who taught me to love books.

—L.M.

The Learning Works, Inc.
P. O. Box 6187
Santa Barbara, CA 93160

Library of Congress Catalog Number: 95-077388
ISBN: 0-88160-278-7

Printed in the United States of America.
Current Printing (last digit): 10 9 8 7 6 5 4 3 2 1

Contents

Lois Lowry at home

Chapter 1
The Writer's Beginning

Eight-year-old Lois sat on the porch of Great-Aunt Kate's house and cradled a fragile china doll against her chest. Her blond hair caught the sunlight as she traced the doll's delicate, hand-painted features with her finger and smoothed its lace-trimmed, hand-embroidered dress.

Lois liked to imagine herself the mother of a real baby, one just as beautiful as the valuable, antique doll she held in her arms. In her mind, she made up stories about the baby—dramatic, tragic, tender stories. Years later, Lois Lowry would craft stories that millions of young people would read and love. For now, however, the words took shape only in Lois's mind.

> *The sunlight fell across the young girl's arm as she rocked, cradling the delicate infant. . . . The tiny creature stirred slightly in her arms, and her eyes were moist as she looked upon it and thought of her husband far away on the battle-field, perhaps never to know his child.* [1]

When it was time for Lois to go home, her indulgent aunt asked if she would like to take the doll with her for a short visit. Lois was thrilled—and very aware of the responsibility that was now hers. With great care, she carried the doll home. As she walked, she sheltered the doll's fragile head in her arms, just as she had seen her mother do with her infant brother Jonny a few years earlier.

Lois's brother Jonny, however, was now an active toddler. Sometime during the baby doll's visit, he grabbed for it and . . . crash! In an instant, the china doll was on the floor, its delicate, hand-painted head in pieces. Lois's baby was "dead"—murdered, actually. In her mind, the young author-to-be continued the mother's dramatic tale.

> *The brutal stranger wrest the infant from her helpless arms.* [2]

Lois was distraught. The china doll was not a gift, only on loan for a short visit. Clearly, the doll must be repaired.

But how? In the small Pennsylvania town where she lived, no one had the skill to restore such a precious antique to its original splendor.

After much searching, Lois's mother found someone in New York City who could repair the doll. She left her two daughters and young son with a trusted babysitter. No one but Lois knew why her mother was making the trip.

In New York, the doll had to stay in a doll hospital for several days. During that time, Lois's mother wrote home to her three children. The letter to Lois was marked "private." In it, her mother wrote, "The baby is doing well, and I will be able to bring her home from the hospital very soon."

Lois, however, had a short memory for minor tragedies. She had already forgotten about the broken baby doll. When she read her mother's letter, she imagined that her mother had gone to New York to adopt or even give birth to a real baby. In this fantasy, her mother had chosen to confide only in Lois. A new story began to form in the young writer's head.

The two sisters met their mother at the train station when she returned from her mysterious trip to the big city. In her arms was a squirming pink bundle. "What's that?" asked the older daughter in amazement. The younger, who had been specially entrusted with the secret, smiled knowingly. . . .[3]

When Lois's mother returned home, her actual arrival was, of course, quite different. The eagerly awaited "squirming pink bundle" was nowhere in sight. In its place was a lifeless china doll. Lois turned pink with embarrassment. She had completely misunderstood her mother's letter. How could she have been so foolish!

In spite of her shame, the budding storyteller began to transform the truth into yet another tale.

> *The little girl, in her excited anticipation of a baby sister, had completely forgotten the doll. How foolish she was. . . .* [4]

Eventually, by turning the incident into fiction, Lois saw the humor in the situation, and her embarrassment began to fade.

The china doll episode is one of Lois Lowry's earliest memories of turning bits and pieces of her life into fiction. And Lois's life, from the very beginning, was full of variety and fascinating events—just like her books.

Chapter 2
The Early Years

Storytelling was a tradition in Lois's family. Lois's father, Robert Hammersberg, had many stories to tell. He grew up in rural Wisconsin, but his family name was not always Hammersberg. Originally, it was Anderson. When these Anderson ancestors first arrived in the United States from Norway, some of them got jobs building the railroad, along with dozens of other Anderson families from Norway. The paymaster, to avoid confusion, asked some of these Andersons to change their names. Many took the names of the Norwegian villages where they had been born. Lois's ancestors took the name of Hammersberg.

As a young man, Robert Hammersberg went to dental school. After graduation, he enlisted in the United States Army. He was assigned to the Dental Corps and eventually stationed in Carlisle, Pennsylvania. There he met the lovely Katharine Landis.

Katharine, the daughter of a bank president, was descended from a long line of Pennsylvania farmers and lawyers. One of her grandfathers had grown up in an Amish home, where religion forbade fancy clothes and discouraged reliance on modern conveniences. This grandfather left the isolated Amish farming community of his birth to further his education, and he never went back. However, his daughter, Katharine's aunt, left a written family record that recalled visits by her Amish uncles and aunts. This record described aunts dressed in plain black dresses, three-cornered black shawls, and little black bonnets. The uncles had bearded faces framed by broad-brimmed hats.

In 1933 Katharine Landis and Robert Hammersberg were married in Fort Benning, Georgia, where Robert was stationed with the U.S. Army. They named their first child, a daughter, Helen Boyd after Katharine's mother, who had died a few years earlier.

Three years later, on March 20, 1937, in Honolulu, Hawaii, their second daughter was born. Robert and Katharine named their new baby Cena after Robert's mother, Cena Ericson Hammersberg.

When the elder Cena heard the news, she flatly refused the honor. She didn't want her granddaughter burdened with such a name. Baby Cena soon became baby Lois Ann, named after her father's two sisters. Eleven months later, Cena Hammersberg traveled halfway across North America and the Pacific Ocean to attend Lois Ann Hammersberg's christening in Hawaii.

Like all army families, the Hammersbergs knew better than to get too settled in one place, for they would soon be moving on. When Lois was two years old, they made the long journey by ship from Hawaii, through the Panama Canal, to New York City for her father's next army assignment.

On the long ocean voyage, Lois complained constantly of the cold. Chilly ocean breezes were an abrupt change for someone who had spent all of her life in the warm tropical climate of Hawaii. Lois also wondered out loud when they would go back home to Hawaii. The answer, as it turned out, was never.

The family arrived in New York City and settled into an apartment in an area of Brooklyn called Bay Ridge. Now, more than fifty years later, Lois can still recall the exact address: 140 87th Street. Her father had the address engraved on gold reproductions of military dog tags for both of his daughters. Lois used this detail from her life in her novel *Autumn Street*, in which the narrator recalls similar identification tags given to her and her sister.

While the Hammersbergs lived in Brooklyn, an exciting event took place in New York City—the 1940 World's Fair. Lois and her family joined the many visitors crowding the fair, and Lois still has two photographs taken that day. One shows two golden-haired children face to face with one of the fair's roving clowns. The older girl boldly reaches out for a handshake. The younger one, Lois, looks on shyly but with interest, holding tightly to her mother's hand. It is a visual image that reflects Lois's later impression of herself as a child. In her view, her older sister Helen was the outgoing, pretty, popular one. Lois, on the other hand, was shy and awkward.

Although the photos of the World's Fair are in black and white, Lois Lowry remembers vividly what she and her sister wore that day. She can still picture the blue of her sister's pinafore, the darker blue of her own jacket, and the red and blue plaid of her skirt. At the age of three, Lois was already noticing and storing sensory details, a clear sign of a writer-in-training.

Later the same day, after the Hammersbergs left the fair, they visited a friend, an elegant woman who lived in a luxurious apartment filled with beautiful—and fragile—knickknacks. Off by herself in a quiet corner of the apartment, surrounded by golden sunlight shining through the windows, Lois twirled around and around. High above her head she held a large paper parasol bought that afternoon at the fair. She felt as elegant as her surroundings. With no one watching, the shy girl could lose herself in her fantasies without feeling awkward.

Suddenly, a crash! The parasol had knocked over one of the many beautiful objects in the room. Joy and exhilaration turned instantly to despair and guilt. Lois felt she had ruined her moment of beauty and embarrassed herself and her parents in front of the elegant woman. Bursting into wild sobs, she buried her head against her father's jacket. Although the grownups tried to comfort her and to assure her they were not upset with her, Lois could not be consoled. Everything had been perfect. Now it was utterly spoiled.

This memory—of great joy mingled with humiliation and the inability to be comforted—has stayed with Lois all of her life.

Eventually, three-year-old Lois managed to put aside the tragedy. She soon turned to a developing interest in letters, words, sentences, and stories.

Without being aware of what she was doing, Lois taught herself to read. She had learned to love books from her mother, a former teacher who read often to her two daughters. Still, it was no small achievement for a three-year-old to master the complicated skill of reading. Lois remembers being thrilled with the realization that she could put letters together to form words, put words together to form sentences, and, better still, put sentences together to make stories.

Soon she was toddling off to nursery school, the only reader in a class of three-year-olds. Her classmates entered enthusiastically into the usual preschool games. Lois particularly remembers one where the children paraded around the room, swinging their arms like elephant trunks. Lois hated this game and would retreat to a corner of the room with a book. She later described herself as "an intellectual snob at the age of three."

Instead of being impressed with this prodigy, the teacher viewed Lois's accomplishment as a problem. She wrote a note to Lois's parents: "Her unusual ability to read and write sets her apart from the other children." The note made it clear that being different was definitely not a plus in the sociable world of nursery school.

At home things were much more fun. Her mother read aloud often, and her father told wonderful stories about his Wisconsin boyhood. Sometimes he recounted his memories of riding on horseback along the banks of a river. Often he delighted Lois by speaking "funny-sounding" Norwegian and describing, with a horribly wrinkled nose, the taste of the pickled fish he relished as a child.

The forces of history, however, soon changed Lois's happy family life. On December 7, 1941, Lois's mother turned on the radio as Lois's father was getting ready to go out. He was dressed in civilian clothes because, like other army doctors and dentists, he did not have to wear a uniform in peacetime. Seconds after he left the house, Lois's mother bolted out the door. What she had heard on the radio made her stop her husband as he was getting into the car. "You've got to come back in and put on your uniform," she cried. "We're at war!"

Japan had bombed the United States Naval Base at Pearl Harbor in Hawaii, and Congress had declared war against Japan. Most of Europe had been at war since 1939, with England and France struggling to hold the line against Germany and its ally, Italy. Since Japan sided with Germany and Italy, the United States was automatically drawn into the European conflict. Thus, within a few days, the United States joined the war on two fronts, in Europe and in the Pacific.

At first, seeing her father in uniform every day was the biggest change the war brought to Lois's life. Soon, however, there was fear that New York, the country's largest city, might be the target of an enemy attack. At all times, Lois and her sister wore the little gold dog tags their father had given them so that they could be identified if the city were bombed and they were separated from their parents.

Before long, there was a much greater upheaval in Lois's life than wearing a gold dog tag and seeing her father in uniform. Like so many other men in 1941, Lois's father was sent off to war.

Chapter 3
At Home in Carlisle

In 1942, when Lois was five years old, her mother, Katharine, was expecting another baby. With her husband away at war, Katharine wanted to be with her family. Once again, she and her two daughters moved, this time to Carlisle, Pennsylvania, Katharine Landis Hammersberg's hometown.

Carlisle was a quiet college town in south central Pennsylvania. This was Lois's home for six years, the longest time she lived in one place until she married and had children of her own.

When the family first moved to Carlisle, Lois, Helen, and their mother stayed with Grandfather Landis at his big family homestead. Later, they moved to a house of their own only half a block away.

Most of Lois's childhood memories are from the days she lived in Carlisle. There she was immediately drawn into her mother's extended family, most of whom warmly welcomed Katharine and her children. Lois adored her grandfather, who returned her affection. Unfortunately, his wife had no such feelings. Grandfather Landis had remarried after his first wife died. His new wife did not like children, and she made no effort to conceal her feelings. She was the one member of the family Lois tried to avoid.

Besides her grandfather, Lois turned to the family cook, Fleta Jordan, for attention and affection. Fleta offered Lois far more warmth than her step-grandmother did. In the kitchen of her grandfather's house, Lois found a listening ear as well as tasty cookies straight from the oven.

For friendship Lois turned to Fleta Jordan's granddaughter, who often visited the house. However, this favorite playmate never came through the front door or played in the front yard. Fleta Jordan and her granddaughter were black, and racial prejudice was widespread in the 1940s. Fleta and her granddaughter were subject to unwritten rules that were common at that time.

Besides Lois's grandfather, other relatives welcomed the young family, especially Lois's three great-aunts, the sisters of her real grandmother. They doted on Lois and on her sister and baby brother, Jonny, who was born in January of 1943. Unlike Lois's step-grandmother, the great-aunts loved having children around and were delighted when Lois came to play. They even shared their treasured possessions with her, including the antique china doll that figured so prominently in those early stories Lois created in her head.

The great-aunts also shared fascinating stories about their youth. They had been known as the beautiful Boyd sisters, and all of them (including Lois's grandmother) had gone to college at a time when few women had that opportunity. After graduating from college, one of the sisters—Mary—did something daring. She went off on her own to New York City, where she violated the standards of the day by engaging in such shocking behavior as smoking cigarettes, wearing trousers, and studying photography! When World War I broke out, Mary and her sister Kate promptly sailed for Europe to aid the war effort by driving ambulances at the battlefront. Lois loved to hear the tales of her great-aunts, but only later in life did she realize how unusually brave and daring these women were, considering the period in which they were raised.

Lois didn't find the men of her family nearly as interesting, although she always enjoyed hearing the story of one great-grandfather who dug his way out of a southern prisoner-of-war camp during the Civil War. On the whole, the Landis men were solid, successful businessmen. Lois's grandfather, a banker, had the distinction of being the inventor of the Christmas Club. This is a savings plan in which people set aside a certain amount of money each week of the year. The money is withdrawn at the end of the year to help pay for holiday expenses. This concept became extremely popular. Many years later, Lois's grandfather's name even turned up on the quiz show "Jeopardy." Contestants had to ask the question that called for the answer, "Bank president Merkel Landis founded this in Pennsylvania."

Besides grandparents and great-aunts, Lois had other relatives in and around Carlisle. They included Katharine's brother, his wife, and their children, who were always a part of family gatherings. In fact, Lois's brother Jonny still remembers this uncle as a father figure during the war years when Robert Hammersberg was home only for brief periods of military leave.

In September of 1942, Lois started first grade at the Franklin Elementary School, a few blocks from her grandfather's house. As Lois recalls it, the school was quite different from today's elementary schools. Teachers stood in front of the class talking for most of the day. Students, with their hands folded, sat at desks that were bolted to the floor.

The classes took no field trips. The school had no library, no gymnasium, and no cafeteria. At lunchtime, Lois, like all the other students, hurried home, hastily gulped down a meal fixed by her mother, and hurried back to school. To Lois's disappointment, art and music classes were given on an irregular basis. Every once in a while an art teacher showed up, told the students to draw something, and abruptly departed. With a similarly un-predictable schedule, a music teacher would arrive with her pitch pipe and conduct the class in a few dull songs. Then she too would disappear for long periods of time.

In spite of all this, Lois liked the first grade, and she loved her teacher, Miss Eddy, who married that year and became Mrs. MacDonnell. All the other teachers in the school were unmarried. In fact, many years later, when Lois was on a lecture tour in South Dakota, a woman introduced herself as Mrs. MacDonnell's daughter. She told Lois that the Carlisle school system had a rule at that time against employing married female teachers. Mrs. MacDonnell had been the first of Carlisle's female teachers to marry.

Despite her affection for Mrs. MacDonnell, first grade had its challenges for Lois. As in nursery school, she was the only student in the class who could read, at least at the beginning of the school year. And, of course, her reading improved steadily, so she was always several steps ahead of her classmates.

She was bored with the simple first-grade readers featuring Dick and Jane and their baby sister Sally. Each page of the reader contained just a few words printed in very large type. A typical page read something like this: "Jane can run. See Jane run. Run, Jane, run." This was not very challenging for someone who had been reading since she was three years old. Outside of school, Lois devoured such classics as *The Five Little Peppers*, which she found in the library of her grandfather's house.

As if Dick and Jane weren't enough to discourage Lois, Mrs. MacDonnell, perhaps in a misguided effort to keep her star reader involved in the class, made Lois the class reading aide. Mrs. MacDonnell told the other children that if they came to a word they didn't know during silent reading, they should ask Lois what the word was. To this day, Lois remembers when the class was reading a story about baby chicks. One by one, each child in the class approached Lois's desk to ask her what a certain word was. The word was *incubator*, one that most first graders would not know. Lois was as embarrassed by the situation as the stumbling readers who came to her for help—maybe even more so.

At the end of first grade, in recognition of her reading skills, Lois was promoted to third grade, skipping second grade entirely. In reading, the tiresome Dick and Jane gave way to such intriguing books as *The Belgian Twins* and a long series based on their relatives: *The Dutch Twins*, *The Scottish Twins*, and so on.

Missing second grade, however, caused new problems for Lois—problems more serious than her boredom with Dick and Jane. The third graders tackled multiplication tables, but Lois had not yet mastered addition and subtraction. Although she eventually "got" it, she never felt quite comfortable with math again. Throughout her school years, it remained her least favorite subject. Like a good student, she dutifully mastered the basics, but she never really believed that she understood what mathematics was all about.

In addition, by skipping second grade, Lois missed the introduction to cursive writing. For a while, she faked a cursive style with her own creative interpretation of the Palmer writing method.

The biggest adjustment Lois had to make in entering the third grade was the change in teachers. Gone was the warmly supportive Mrs. MacDonnell. For most of the remaining elementary school years, Lois endured a series of stern women who communicated no love of children or teaching. These women were not necessarily mean, but they were distant and not particularly enthusiastic about their jobs. Their students, responding in kind, expressed little enthusiasm for these teachers.

Still, Lois enjoyed many things about school. In addition to reading and writing, she loved drawing. One day, the fifth-grade teacher announced that as part of their study of the westward movement in United States history, the class would create a mural of a wagon train.

Enthusiastically, Lois envisioned her contribution to the mural. She decided she would draw pioneer children walking alongside the wagons. This would be great fun, and Lois eagerly anticipated the day the class would begin working on the mural.

When the time drew near, however, the teacher called Lois aside and told her that since she was one of the best artists in the class, she was to have a special assignment. She was to draw the oxen that pulled the wagons. Oxen did not interest Lois nearly as much as people. Disappointed, she did what was asked of her, unable to muster the courage to voice her preference.

Naturally, Lois, who found it difficult to speak up for herself in school, almost never misbehaved. There was, however, one memorable exception. In fourth grade, she and a girl named Donna wrote a nasty note to a girl named

Ruthie. Lois was caught. Donna was not. A loyal friend, Lois refused to tattle on Donna.

After school, Lois had to face the consequences of her actions alone. Standing by the desk of the stern-faced teacher, unable to look her in the eye for more than a few seconds at a time, Lois focused instead on the teacher's dress, dark with white squiggles. Through her tear-filled eyes, the squiggles seemed to be moving on their own, like tiny worms. Perhaps Lois's stomach felt full of worms, too. Certainly, the uncomfortable situation convinced her that she never wanted to be on the bad side of her teachers again. From then on, Lois carefully maintained her good-girl image.

After school, Lois played with friends in the neighborhood. For several years, her best neighborhood friend was a girl who lived just a few houses away. At school the two girls never acknowledged each other. This friend was a year ahead of Lois, and children in different classes simply didn't mix. At home, however, they played together happily, sometimes joining other neighborhood children as they roller-skated up and down the brick sidewalks of Carlisle, over bumps caused by tree roots heaving up through the bricks. Other times, they played hopscotch on the same bumpy sidewalks or rode their bicycles around the neighborhood.

Although Lois kept busy with school and her friends, the focus of her life in Carlisle was at home.

Chapter 4
Home Life in Wartime

Even with her father away and the world at war, Lois had a happy childhood. Many of the good times she shared with her sister Helen. Both were great movie fans and enthusiastic readers of magazines like *Modern Screen* and *Photoplay*, which provided information about Holly-wood stars. The sisters had a large collection of these fan magazines and pored over them for gossip about their favorite actors and actresses.

Lois liked Jeanne Crain and Cornel Wilde. Helen pre-ferred June Allyson and Van Johnson. The sisters made a point of learning everything they could about these stars. They knew the names of their wives or husbands and children. They knew what the stars' houses were like and whether they had pets. At night, in their beds, the two sisters had whispered conversations about "their" movie stars.

Both girls were also fans of popular music. Once a week, they tuned in to a radio program called "Your Hit Parade" to listen to the top-selling songs of the week. Helen had a favorite singer named Vaughn Monroe. His most well-known song was called "Racing with the Moon." Lois used to drive her big sister crazy by crooning the song with exaggerated o's, so that it sounded like "Racing with the Mooooon." During this period, Robert Hammersberg, home on leave from the army, managed to acquire a larger-than-life, cardboard-backed, color photo of Monroe, which had been in the display window of a local music store. For several years this poster was propped up in the girls' bedroom.

When Lois and Helen were not playing or swooning over movie stars, they had chores to do. To aid the war effort, people at home did whatever they could. Sometimes Lois flattened tin cans for the weekly scrap metal collection at school. Other times she helped her mother in the kitchen by adding yellow coloring to the tasteless, white butter substitute.

Sometimes the family went shopping, using the required rationing coupons. To cope with wartime shortages, families were only allowed a small quantity of some items each month. Every time Lois's family purchased meat, coffee, bacon, sugar, butter, or gasoline, they had to present a coupon from a ration booklet. When the family reached its monthly limit on any one of those items, they could buy no more until the next month's ration booklet arrived.

Like most families, the Hammersbergs were happy to aid the war effort. It was a way for civilians to help their country win the war and bring their loved ones home faster. Other than these small efforts, however, the war seemed far away. Lois does remember one bit of war-related excitement that occurred when a German soldier escaped from a prisoner-of-war camp near Carlisle. He stole clothes off the clothesline in the yard next to Lois's. Was Lois frightened? No, she was jealous. She longed for something exciting to happen to her family.

Despite the war, there was plenty of time for fun. On Saturday afternoons, the neighborhood children went to the theater on High Street to see the latest cowboy movie. Lois's favorites were the movies starring the husband and wife team of Roy Rogers and Dale Evans, with the Sons of the Pioneers singing "Tumbling Tumbleweeds" as the final credits rolled.

Lois also remembers Saturday evenings in spring and fall when the neighborhood children hid in the bushes outside the gymnasium of the local college. From there they spied on the elegantly dressed college couples as they arrived for formal dances. When school closed for the summer, Sunday evenings brought outdoor concerts to the college grounds. Lois's family sprawled on blankets and enjoyed the music under the stars.

Summer also brought a change of scenery when the family spent time at a home that Lois's grandmother had bought. It was only fifteen miles from Carlisle, so the short car trip didn't use up too many gas rations. The summer home, really a converted nineteenth-century mill, rose three stories high. It had thick stone walls and mammoth fireplaces, and there was a lake not far away.

The grounds of the Landis summer home also held a temptation, a crumbling old blacksmith shop. Lois and the other children were warned to stay away from it. Snakes lurked there, they were told. Usually obedient children, they longed for a summer adventure. Sometimes they would tiptoe as close to the blacksmith shop as they dared. When their imaginations convinced them that they could hear the rattle of a rattlesnake, they would run off screaming with fear and excitement.

In the summer evenings, everyone—grownups and children alike—gathered at the general store a short distance from the mill. The grownups gossiped. The teenagers flirted. The children played tag and ate ice cream. During one summer, Lois noticed that her sister Helen had left the ranks of the boisterous children and joined the whispering teenagers. Lois still remembers the confusion and sadness she felt as her sister began this transition to another stage in her life.

Although Lois took part in neighborhood and family activities, she saw herself as a shy and unathletic girl. For team games, she was always the last one chosen. Actually, she preferred the company of a book to that of children playing athletic games.

Her love of books drew her to the public library, a dimly lit building with high, vaulted ceilings. To Lois, the librarian reigned like a goddess. When Lois brought the books she had chosen to the check-out desk, the librarian performed some mysterious ceremony with the tools of her trade. Then, miraculously, the books were Lois's to bring home and to relish until it was time to return them.

In the summer, Lois often visited the library two and three times a day until the stern librarian informed her that she must limit herself to one trip per day. After that, Lois chose her books carefully, always selecting the thickest ones she could find so they would last through the day.

The librarian also kept a close watch on what Lois read. When Lois was ten years old, she discovered a book called *A Tree Grows in Brooklyn*. The title sounded intriguing, and Lois remembered that she had once lived in Brooklyn. The book seemed perfect for her.

She took it to the check-out desk, but the librarian informed Lois that this was a book for adults, not children. Even so, Lois insisted on checking out the book. By the time she arrived home, the librarian had already telephoned her mother to warn her that Lois had checked out a book that was not suitable for children. Katharine Hammersberg responded politely but without concern. She had read the book herself and recalled nothing in it that would harm her ten-year-old daughter.

Lois loved *A Tree Grows in Brooklyn*. After reading it, she wanted, like Francie, to grow up in a bustling city slum and make a better life for herself using sheer grit and determination. This was only one of Lois's fantasies.

Another of Lois's fantasies was also based on one of her favorite books, *The Yearling*, by Marjorie Kinnan Rawlings. Katharine Hammersberg had read the book to Lois and Helen when they were nine and twelve years old. The edition Lois's mother read had dramatic illustrations by N. C. Wyeth that fascinated Lois. At night, after her mother finished reading, she would leave the book in Lois's room. Frequently, Lois crept out of bed to study the illustrations, losing herself in the scenes.

One illustration in particular fascinated her. Called "The Burial of Fodder-Wing," it showed a bearded man carrying a small casket followed by a sad procession of mourners. The drooping foliage of weeping trees filled the top half of the page. The illustration appealed to Lois's imagination. She fantasized about making her home in a Florida swamp, having a wild deer for a pet, and befriending a poor disabled boy who would die young so that Lois could mourn at his grave.

The deaths of fictional children intrigued Lois, and so did a true story her mother told her about something that had happened years before. Three sisters had been found shot to death in the woods near Carlisle. "Babes in the Wood" the local newspaper had called them. Who were they? Lois wondered. Who killed them? Why? How old were they? She wondered whether one of them was ten, just her age when she heard the story.

Lois's mother couldn't recall any of the details. Instead, Lois's research skills helped her answer her own questions. In the dusty recesses of the library, after much hunting, Lois found the story in an old newspaper. As it turned out, the three "Babes in the Wood" were not babes at all, but teenagers. According to the newspaper, the girls' nomadic mother and her boyfriend grew tired of carting three teenaged girls around with them. The adults shot the girls and left them in the woods. The girls were buried in the same cemetery as Lois's grandmother and, after many requests, Lois finally convinced her mother to take her there. They found the tombstone, "Babes in the Wood," just like in the newspaper headline.

Lois mulled over the tragedy. Like the china doll incident, it appealed to her sense of drama. Eventually, she turned her storytelling skills to this real event, making up the details until she was satisfied with her half-true and half-invented tale.

More raw material for Lois's imagination came from the wonderful stories she heard about her father's sister, her Aunt Lois. As a young nurse, Aunt Lois had joined the Red Cross and traveled across China and Siberia to get to Russia during the Russian Revolution, which started in 1917. Aunt Lois thrilled her namesake with the story of riding on horseback behind a Bolshevik rebel soldier and being shot at by soldiers loyal to the czar.

To young Lois this was not only an exciting tale, but also raw material for her vivid imagination. Before long she had concocted a story in which her aunt was involved in a tragic love affair with the soldier. This dramatic tale came from only one fact, the horseback ride.

It wasn't long before Lois began writing down stories like the ones she had invented for years in her head. By the fourth or fifth grade, she knew she wanted to be a writer.

Her teachers encouraged her and praised what they saw of her writing. Lois, however, did not usually show what she wrote to anyone. Unfortunately, because her family moved so much and things were regularly discarded, all of Lois's childhood writing has disappeared.

In 1948, at the end of sixth grade, Lois's family made an important decision. World War II had ended three years earlier, but Lois's father was still stationed in Japan with the American military forces occupying that country. The family saw him only when he returned to the United States for brief leaves. Now, Lois, her mother, her sister, and her brother were to join him in Japan. The family would be together again.

Lois was thrilled. For six years, she had lived without her father. Soon her whole family would be together. Also, Japan sounded much more exciting than Carlisle. In her last few months of sixth grade, Lois gave oral reports on Japan, emphasizing its exotic aspects. Without actually saying so, she managed to suggest that she would soon be off on a romantic adventure while her classmates remained in dull Carlisle.

Sayonara, Carlisle. Hello, Japan.

Chapter 5
On the Move

Before Lois could embark on her journey to exotic Japan, she had to endure the unpleasant experience of being inoculated against a host of diseases. Typhus, cholera, typhoid fever, yellow fever—the list seemed endless, and so did the summer of 1948. Lois spent much of it alternately in a doctor's office being jabbed with large needles, and in bed at home suffering from the raging fevers that came as a reaction to the shots.

As the end of summer approached, Lois and her family boarded a ship in New York. Ahead of them was a month-long ocean voyage down the east coast of the United States, through the Panama Canal, and across the Pacific Ocean. For the first week, Lois was violently seasick. The rest of the time she was bored. The wharves of Yokohama finally loomed into sight, however, and with them came the start of a new chapter in Lois's life.

After the ride to their new home through crowded, war-torn Tokyo, life in Japan didn't seem very different from life in Carlisle. As dependents of the United States Army, the Hammersbergs lived in an area of Tokyo inhabited only by Americans. A fence separated the neighborhood from the rest of the city. Inside the fence was a village that looked as if it could have been picked up anywhere in the United States and transported intact to Japanese soil. The houses were American, the neighbors were American, and the small movie theater showed American films. There was a church, a library, and an elementary school, all indistinguishable from any in the United States, thousands of miles away. Appropriately, this miniature U.S.A. was named Washington Heights.

Why, Lois puzzled, had her family traveled all this way to live in surroundings just like the ones they had left behind? Why, she asked her mother, weren't they living among Japanese people, where they could learn about the real Japan? Her mother told her that they lived in Washington Heights because it was safe, familiar, and comfortable.

Safe and comfortable didn't interest Lois nearly as much as new and unfamiliar. Many times her curiosity drew her out of Washington Heights. Sneaking out the back gate of the compound without her parents' knowledge, she rode her bicycle down a hill and into a part of Tokyo called Shibuya, an area of shops, theaters, and street vendors.

In Shibuya Lois found a splendid array of new sights, smells, and sounds. Young children, dressed in vibrant shades of pink, orange, and red, toddled along beside their parents. Older schoolchildren roamed in groups, easily identifiable by their somber, dark blue uniforms. Lois's nose filled with the smells of fish, fertilizer, and the charcoal being used to cook finger-food on open fires. Strange music and loud shouting in a language she was just beginning to understand accosted Lois's ears. Beneath the music and the shouting came the clatter of wooden things: wooden shoes on pavement, wooden sticks, and the wooden wheels of carts. The vivid colors, the pungent odors, and the lively sounds contrasted sharply with Lois's own quiet life.

Lois observed all this activity without ever speaking to anyone. Shyly, she watched Japanese children playing near a school. She would have liked to join their games or talk to them, but her shyness kept her an outsider.

On one of Lois's solitary excursions, an older woman approached her. She stroked Lois's blond hair, which was an unusual color among the black-haired Japanese people. Then she spoke to Lois in Japanese. With her beginner's understanding of the language, Lois thought the woman said *kirai-desu*, meaning she didn't like Lois. Confused and embarrassed, Lois wondered what she had done to offend this stranger. Moments later, she realized her mistake. The woman had actually said *kirei-desu*, "pretty." Lois had mistaken a compliment for an insult. Quickly she turned, but the woman had disappeared. It was too late to smile or to say "thank you."

With the other American students from Washington Heights, Lois rode a bus across Tokyo to the English-speaking Meguro School. The driver, a Japanese man, took great pains at Christmastime to adorn the inside of the bus with brightly colored paper decorations. Though gaudy and cheap, they were nonetheless festive. Even at the age of twelve, Lois understood what an extraordinary gesture this man had made. Like most Japanese, he was almost certainly not Christian and, also like most Japanese, he probably had little money to spare in the aftermath of the war. Even so, he had given both his time and his money to help these conquering foreigners celebrate their holiday.

One day, when the bus was full, a group of rowdy boys, probably more out of high spirits than malice, began to tear the decorations to pieces and scatter them around the bus. Lois saw the look on the driver's face as he watched his hard work torn apart. Though horrified, she said nothing to try to stop the destruction. How could shy, quiet Lois Hammersberg confront such rowdy, noisy boys?

Yet the shyness that made Lois quiet and content to be alone did not keep her from having friends. Her visits to Shibuya sometimes included the company of five or six classmates from the Meguro School. All of them wore the American uniform of blue jeans and sneakers, and all of them had been strictly warned by their parents not to touch native foods. The water was not purified, the milk was not pasteurized, and the vegetables had been fertilized with human waste.

The adventurous—and ravenous—children ignored the advice of their parents. They meandered through Shibuya, happily slurping popsicles made with unpurified water and gobbling up the many foods that were for sale, though Lois herself drew the line at sampling dried grasshoppers.

Shibuya provided an interesting and lively playground for these American junior high school students, but other sights in Tokyo were disturbing. The city was still recovering from the bombings of World War II. Only four or five years earlier, people's homes had been destroyed and families had been torn apart. As Lois walked around Tokyo, she often saw evidence of the war's devastation. Some Japanese families still lived in huge wooden packing crates or in shacks made from sheets of tin. Here the reality of war felt very different from what Lois had known in the safe surroundings of Carlisle, Pennsylvania.

Even when Lois got away from Tokyo, she saw reminders of the war. For two summers, she went alone by train to the city of Kure and from there took a boat to the island of Eta Jima in the Inland Sea of Southern Honshu. There she visited her best friend from seventh grade, whose father had been transferred to the island. On Eta Jima, barricades blocked off part of the forest, and signs were posted warning that unexploded land mines had yet to be cleared away.

Lois enjoyed exploring her new environment, but the best part of living in Japan was having her father at home. Growing up in Carlisle during the war years without her father around had made Lois feel different. Now her life felt more normal with her whole family together again.

Lois admired—and sometimes envied—her big sister Helen, now an attractive and outgoing high school student. Helen even had a steady boyfriend named Jack. A football star, he gave Helen a little silver football on a chain to wear around her neck. Though Lois herself was too young to date, once in a while Helen and Jack would take her with them to a sports event or a movie. Lois marveled that a popular teenage girl would allow her little sister to tag along on dates.

In 1950, after two years in Japan, another war intruded on the Hammersbergs' family life. United States troops joined a United Nations force sent to resolve a conflict between North and South Korea. Because Korea is so close to Japan, American military families in Japan were sent home as a safety measure. Lois's father had to stay behind, but Lois, her sister and brother, and her mother returned once again to Pennsylvania.

Chapter 6
Stateside Again

The Hammersbergs sailed from Yokohama to San Francisco and then traveled across the United States by train. In Chicago Lois's mother and little brother left the train and went on to Wisconsin to visit Robert Hammersberg's family. Lois and Helen, ages thirteen and sixteen, continued on the train alone from Chicago to Harrisburg, Pennsylvania, where their grandparents met them. On the train, the sisters pretended they were their favorite movie actresses, Jeanne Crain and June Allyson, traveling together from Hollywood to New York.

The Hammersbergs settled in Carlisle just in time for Lois to enter the ninth grade with the same classmates she had left behind two years earlier. Unfortunately for Lois, things had changed. Her classmates had formed new friendships and new groups, and Lois was not a part of them. A more outgoing girl might have found a place for herself in a group, but this kind of effort did not come easily to Lois. She waited for people to come to her, and when they didn't, she felt left out. In the place that had been home longer than any other place in her lifetime, she was not part of things anymore. She was an outsider.

Years later, Lois recalled these feelings when she wrote her second book, *Find a Stranger, Say Good-bye*. In the book, a woman who became pregnant at the age of fifteen and then gave her baby up for adoption explains her loneliness at being a new girl in town. Although Lois never experienced a teenage pregnancy, she had experienced the loneliness of being an outsider. She expressed the intensity of those feelings through her writing.

Before long, it was time to leave Carlisle again. Lois's father came home from Japan with a new assignment. He took his family back to New York City, this time to an army base located on an island in New York Harbor. Governors Island was, of course, much smaller than Japan, but life there was similar to life in Washington Heights. Inhabited only by army families, the island had its own movie theater, its own shops, and its own elementary school—but no high school.

Lois, who was about to enter tenth grade, had her choice of several New York City public high schools.

More accurately, her parents had their choice of those schools. They chose Curtis High School, a public high school on Staten Island, the most suburban of New York City's five boroughs. Of all the New York high schools, it would be, they assumed, most like the schools Lois had attended previously.

With no ferry from Governors Island to Staten Island, Lois had to take a ferry to Manhattan and then another ferry from there to Staten Island, an unusual commute for any high school student.

Curtis High School was not like the other schools Lois had attended, as her parents had hoped. The school was huge, and Lois knew no one. Many of the students seemed like streetwise juvenile delinquents to her. By the end of the year, Lois was desperate to leave Curtis High.

Her best friend at the high school was going off to boarding school, and Lois begged her parents to send her somewhere, anywhere, other than Curtis High School. Though her parents could not afford to send her to boarding school, they did agree to let her commute to a private girls' school in Brooklyn.

Packer Collegiate Institute emphasized academics and, equally important for Lois, was much smaller than Curtis High. With only forty-six students in her class, Lois experienced two wonderful years at Packer. Having attended four schools in five years, she finally found one where she felt at home.

In addition to the importance placed on learning, Packer's teachers were committed to taking advantage of the cultural life of New York City. The French teacher took

Lois and other students to see a French movie. Another teacher took students to the opera. The Latin teacher invited a group of girls to go to a concert at her church and afterwards treated them to tea at her apartment.

These excursions opened up new vistas to Lois, whose parents were not particularly interested in the cultural events that New York City had to offer. Lois herself had made sure that she experienced the real Japan. Now her teachers at Packer made sure that she experienced the best of New York.

Although Lois felt she had finally found a school where she could flourish, she remained quiet and reticent. Sometimes she envied the "cheerleader" types and secretly wished she could be like them and like her pretty and popular older sister, who always seemed at ease with people. To Lois, it seemed that Helen was always May Queen while Lois won the Latin Prize, all the time yearning to be May Queen, too.

Never part of a crowd, Lois instead cultivated a few close friends. Since Packer was an all-girls school, she had little opportunity to meet boys. Dates were limited to a few weekend trips to attend dances at a Connecticut boys' school. Lois avoided joining clubs and taking part in social activities. She preferred spending her leisure time reading and writing.

Periodically a school guidance counselor would call Lois in for a chat and remind her that colleges looked not only at applicants' grades, but at their extracurricular activities as well. The counselor would urge her to join a few clubs to impress the colleges she would like to attend.

Lois would solemnly promise to join the French Club or the chorus or to try out for the school play. Then she would go home to her books and her writing, convinced that at least one college would be eager to admit a student who was well-read and could write fluently, even if she didn't have extracurricular activities.

English was Lois's favorite subject at Packer, and her teachers readily recognized her talent. During her senior year, Lois gave her English teacher a poem she had written. The teacher graded it A+ and wrote a note saying, "Be sure to go on writing. I think there's a real chance you might do something with it."

Even Lois's classmates viewed her as a writer-to-be. Under her senior picture in the yearbook was the prediction "Future Novelist."

Lois knew she needed to find a college that would look with favor on an applicant who knew she wanted to be a writer and who dedicated herself to that goal. Surely there were colleges that didn't expect every applicant to play the tuba or lead the basketball team to victory. The question was, which college was right for Lois?

Chapter 7
College Days

Her parents had the answer. Although they lived in New York at the time, like all military personnel who moved around a lot, they had chosen one state to be their permanent legal residence. That state was Pennsylvania, and one of the benefits of being a legal resident of Pennsylvania was that Lois could go to Penn State for a reduced tuition. Helen had enrolled at Penn State two years earlier, and Lois's parents expected Lois to follow her sister there.

However, two years at a school where teachers encouraged her to think for herself had had an effect on Lois.

She had definite ideas about where she wanted to go to college. She preferred a small, private college, even though it would cost considerably more than Penn State. Although Lois was neither stubborn nor argumentative, she was determined.

Knowing that her parents would not pay for her to go to a private college, Lois applied for a scholarship to Pembroke, part of Brown University, in Providence, Rhode Island. On the basis of the writing awards she had won in high school, Pembroke granted Lois a scholarship and accepted her into the creative writing program. That was just where she wanted to be.

Her parents were not pleased that Lois had disregarded their choice of a college for her. However, since she was not asking them for more money than Penn State would have cost, they could not forbid her to go. Instead, they found other ways to express their displeasure.

By September of 1954, Lois's parents had moved to Washington, D.C. While many Pembroke freshmen were being enthusiastically delivered to their dormitories by proud parents, Lois got on a train to make the seven-hour ride by herself from Washington to Providence. Not once during the two years she spent at Brown did her parents come to visit.

At Brown, Lois enrolled in a special honors program for writing. Periodically she met with her advisor, a plump, pink-faced professor whose job was to help Lois grow as a writer. The advisor always had a good word to say about Lois's writing, but he was more critical than her elementary and high school teachers had been.

He admitted that her grammar was flawless. She definitely knew how to make her subjects and verbs agree and where to put her commas. He also found her writing fluent. She certainly could string words and sentences together in a pleasing way.

However, he had some reservations about the content of her writing. Lois had always had a fondness for tragedy, cultivated long ago by her mother's reading of *The Yearling*. In her college years, she specialized in sad, tender stories about children whose dogs had died. The professor suggested that to grow as a writer, she needed to experience more of life. What experience was she lacking? Lois wondered. Perhaps grief, the advisor proposed. Lois admitted to herself that he was right. She had never experienced real grief, nor did she want to.

If grief was not available to her, the professor suggested, perhaps Lois might explore love. Love, he implied, was very close to grief. Now Lois felt confident. Of course she knew about love. She had experienced her first real romance the summer before coming to Brown. While working at a resort in the Pocono Mountains in Pennsylvania, she had met a young man who was studying for the ministry. The two of them shared a tender summer romance. Yes, love was definitely something Lois knew about. Certainly she knew more about it than this ancient professor.

Having convinced herself that she had little to learn from her writing advisor, Lois ended each meeting with him in a similar way. When the time was up, she rose to leave, politely thanking her advisor for the A on her latest paper, for in spite of his reservations about her lack of experience, he always gave her A's, a tribute to the remarkable fluency of her writing. As Lois closed the door behind her, she also closed her mind to any advice the professor had offered.

Although she paid little regard to her advisor's suggestions, Lois did work hard on her writing. However, it was not the sole, or even the most important, focus of her college days. For the first time, she had a social life.

Living in a dormitory with a group of women her own age meant Lois was no longer a loner. When she and her friends were not in class, they sat around the dormitory, playing bridge for hours on end and knitting argyle socks for their boyfriends.

In the evenings, they wound their hair into tight little pin curls. In the morning, they brushed out the curls and fluffed them into halos around their heads. During the day, they periodically ran their fingers through their hair to keep it fluffy.

Many women who attended college in the 1950s believed the most successful coeds were the ones who went out every Saturday night. A young woman who had frequent dates would soon be wearing some young man's fraternity pin. Later she'd sport an engagement ring on the third finger of her left hand. At this point, she was well on her way to the ultimate goal—marriage to an educated man with a promising future.

Attitudes have changed since the 1950s, and women as well as men think of college as a place to get an education, not a wedding ring. Lois regrets that although she can still name the friends who wore fraternity pins on their cashmere sweaters, she cannot recall what subject any of them majored in or what, if any, career goals they had.

Even then, however, not every woman in college concentrated on dating. One woman in Lois's dormitory wore jeans instead of skirts, didn't play bridge or curl her hair, and never had a date on Saturday night. She was pleasant and studious, but Lois, along with the twelve others in the small, shared house, found it easy to ignore someone so different.

For Lois, who was finally comfortable in social situations, Brown offered a feast. With 3,000 men to 700 women, there were enough men interested in dating Lois to keep her busy every Saturday night. Before long, she wore a fraternity pin. An engagement ring soon followed. Before the end of her second year at Brown, she had the marriage proposal so many of her friends dreamed of having.

Now, when Lois looks back on those years, she feels she locked herself into one relationship too soon, without enjoying a variety of dating experiences. At the time, however, she felt she was fulfilling a dream shared by many college women in the 1950s. After having a date every Saturday night, she was getting married.

Fellow student and fiancé Donald Grey Lowry was two years older than Lois and would graduate from Brown in the spring. He wanted the two of them to marry right away. He didn't want Lois to stay at Pembroke for another two years. Lois agreed. In June of 1956, after two years of college, she left Brown University for good. Soon, dressed in a swirling white gown and veil, Lois Ann Hammersberg became Mrs. Donald Lowry.

Chapter 8
Joy and Sorrow

Donald Lowry was an officer in the United States Navy, so once again Lois was on the move. In the first seven years of their marriage, they lived in five different states. From their first home in San Diego, California, they moved to Connecticut, where their first child, a daughter named Alix, was born in 1958. A year later they settled in Florida, where Lois gave birth to their son, Grey. The family celebrated Alix's second birthday and Grey's first in Charleston, South Carolina, and then moved to Cambridge, Massachusetts, the next year. Donald, now out of the navy, planned to attend Harvard Law School.

Cambridge was a charming, quaint, and, as it turned out, expensive city across the Charles River from Boston. Lois was appalled at the high rents. With Donald in law school, money would be tight. To help out with expenses, Lois took on two part-time jobs in addition to the full-time job of caring for two small children.

For one job, Lois typed manuscripts for a professor at Harvard University. Fortunately, she could do this at home while the children napped or slept at night. Her other job, however, was as a sales clerk in the stationery department of the Harvard Coop, a large store run by the university. For this job, Lois had to hire a babysitter to stay at home with Alix and Grey. When she deducted the cost of the child care from her salary, she earned about fifty cents an hour.

As if two jobs and mothering didn't keep her busy enough, Lois also started taking courses at Harvard. Being in the university setting made her acutely aware that she had not finished college, so she added that to her list of things to do. Wife, mother, employee, and student—it was too much. After having her third child, a daughter named Kristin, Lois quit her two jobs and stopped taking classes. For the next several years, she devoted herself to being a wife and mother.

While living in Cambridge, Lois received painful news from her sister Helen. Although as a teenager Lois had envied her sister, she had outgrown her envy after college when their lives took similar turns. Helen had married right out of college and now had three young children, just like Lois. Their similar circumstances brought them closer in one way but kept them apart physically. Helen had married an army officer and moved to Germany and then to Texas. Instead of being two sisters taking their six children to the playground together, Lois and Helen were two sisters separated by thousands of miles.

Helen wrote to Lois that she had been diagnosed with cancer. There was a good chance that she would not live to see her children—ages two, four, and six—grow up.

The sisters began writing regularly to each other. Eventually, Helen was hospitalized in Washington, D.C., close enough to Cambridge for Lois to visit. At the time, Lois was pregnant again, and her doctor urged her not to travel, especially under such upsetting circumstances. The emotional strain of her sister's illness might be harmful for her and her baby. Lois's parents also urged her not to come to Washington. They were taking care of Helen's children and making frequent visits to the hospital, and they felt they couldn't cope with Lois if she became too emotional over her sister's illness.

The doctors predicted that Helen might live another six months, so Lois stayed home in Cambridge and promised herself that when the new baby was old enough to travel, she would go to Washington to see her sister.

Shortly after Benjamin, her fourth child, was born, Lois received a card from Helen that made her weep. Her sister's shaky handwriting showed clearly how weak she had become. Four weeks later, Helen died. Lois never made it to Washington.

To this day, Lois regrets that she didn't go to see her

sister before she died. Years later, she used this personal tragedy as the basis of her first book, *A Summer to Die*. It is about two sisters, one of whom is dying of cancer.

In 1963, the year after Helen's death, Lois Hammersberg Lowry turned twenty-six. She had four children, all under the age of five, and a husband graduating from Harvard Law School. She had achieved everything expected of a 1950s middle-class woman, but where was the writer she had always wanted to be?

Chapter 9
Motherhood and College

When Donald graduated from Harvard Law School, the family moved to Portland, Maine. After years as a wanderer, Lois was finally settled, and she remained settled for the next fourteen years. Her new home was a large old farmhouse on twenty-two acres of land close to downtown Portland. The rural setting was perfect for raising four children and their extensive collection of pets.

The Lowry children, all blond and blue-eyed, were funny, smart, and full of energy. Lois adored them, and she loved being a mother. When the children were small, she did a lot of "elephant marching" with them, playing the same game she had despised as a preschooler. She also attended her share of committee meetings at their schools. She did what was expected of a mother and wife in the 1960s, but she missed her reading and writing.

Naturally, Lois told her children stories. Like most mothers, she also nagged them to clean their rooms and eat their vegetables. Still, when they forgot to clean or pushed their peas and carrots around their plates, she didn't mind. Sometimes she made rules, like "Everyone over seven has to make their own bed." The three older children ignored her. Benjamin, who had just turned seven and was very proud of it, dutifully made his bed every day. When he realized that it wasn't that much fun and that his mother didn't seem to care if the rule was obeyed or not, he stopped. Benjamin also tried valiantly to eat his asparagus, which he hated, until his brother and sisters told him that their mother only pretended to care whether they ate their vegetables.

Although Lois may have let discipline slide in smaller matters, in larger ones she taught her children important lessons—lessons of responsibility and persistence. When her older son, Grey, was twelve he wanted a horse of his own. Lois and her husband told Grey that he could have a horse if he fenced in the pasture. If not, he would have no place to keep the horse. Determined to have a horse, Grey began the daunting task of building a fence. The job required going into the woods and cutting down trees for fence posts, digging post holes in the rocky Maine soil, hauling the posts to the holes, and setting them. At first

Grey's friends helped, but they soon lost interest in the arduous task. For one whole summer, Grey dug and cut and hauled and set. He earned his horse, and he learned a valuable lesson about work and responsibility in the process. His mother believed strongly that young people learned more from their own experiences than from being told what to do by adults. Grey certainly did.

Not every challenge of raising her children was a triumph for Lois. Looking back, there are some things she would have done differently. She wishes she had saved the money to send her older daughter, Alix, to a different school. Alix was a brilliant student and a free thinker. As a junior in high school, Alix came home one day puzzled because she had not been asked to join the National Honor Society. This distinction was extended to very few juniors, but Alix felt she deserved it because of her outstanding academic record. A few days later, Alix asked a favorite teacher if he knew why she had not been picked. Reluctantly, he admitted that some teachers didn't choose her because they felt she acted as if she knew more than the teachers.

A year later, as a senior, Alix was invited into the society. She declined to join. Lois received an outraged call from the school. Her daughter was the first person in the history of the school to turn down this great honor. To make matters worse, the names of the honorees had already been given to the newspaper. Lois expressed her sympathy for the school's dilemma but made it clear that the decision was Alix's, not hers.

She was, however, curious about the reasons for Alix's

decision. Alix explained that she had checked out the society and felt that it didn't do anything. It just looked good on college applications. Since Alix had already been accepted at a college, she thought there was no point in joining the society. Lois supported her daughter completely, but she wondered if Alix would have been happier at a school where the teachers gave students like Alix more support and encouragement—like Lois herself had found at Packer.

When Lois's youngest child, Benjamin, started school, Lois went back to school, too. Always self-conscious about having not finished college, she began taking classes at the University of Southern Maine. In the afternoon, she and her children would sit around a big table in the kitchen doing their homework. The children often wondered aloud why their mother seemed to worry more about her assignments than they did about theirs.

Going to school part-time, Lois spent four years finishing the two years of college she had missed. In 1972 she got her B.A. degree. Then she started working on her master's degree. While she was pursuing her master's, a friend who ran a small publishing company in Maine asked her to write two textbooks, *Black American Literature* (published in 1973) and *Literature of the American Revolution* (published in 1974). Lois now says that an African American should have been given the job of writing the first book. However, she wanted to write, so she took the job.

While Lois was studying literature in graduate school, she took a course in photography to get some credits she needed. To her surprise, she enjoyed it very much. She especially liked experimenting with light and composing a photograph so that all the elements of a picture were arranged just the way she wanted them. She realized that these two things were closely related to writing. When you write, you choose to shed light only on certain aspects of a situation, and then you arrange (compose) events to tell the story you want to tell.

Lois never did finish the work for her master's degree. While she was taking courses, she began writing articles and selling them to newspapers and magazines. Often she took the photographs to go with the articles. She was doing what she had always wanted to do. She decided to stop working on her master's degree in order to devote herself to her writing.

Eventually, in addition to nonfiction articles, she began to write short stories. Some of these stories appeared in well-known national magazines. Most of her stories were based on her memories of childhood. Here is how one story began:

> *It was morning, early, barely light, cold for November. I was nine and the war was over. At home, in the bed next to mine, my older sister still slept, adolescent, her blonde hair streaming over the edge of the sheet. I sat shyly in the front seat next to the stranger who was my father, my blue-jeaned legs pulled up under the too-large wool shirt I was wearing, making a bosom of my knees.*

"Daddy," I said, the title coming uncertainly,
"I've never gone hunting before. What if I don't
know what to do?" [5]

The story was based on something that really happened when Lois's father was home on leave from the army at the end of World War II. Lois was beginning to turn her life into art, and others were beginning to recognize the artistry in her writing.

Chapter 10
One Dream Broken
and Another Realized

In the mid-1970s, an editor from a publishing company in Boston wrote to Lois and asked if she had thought of writing a novel for young readers. Encouraged by the editor's confidence in her writing, Lois sat down and wrote her first novel. She called it *A Summer to Die*. Losing her sister to cancer some fifteen years earlier provided Lois with the basis for this story.

Published in 1977, *A Summer to Die* earned reviewers'

wholehearted praise. Two of them called it a "remark-able" first novel. Perhaps more remarkable was how long it had taken Lois Lowry to do what she always wanted to do. Still, the fulfillment of her dream cost her more than she had anticipated. Her marriage of twenty-one years ended the same year her first book was published.

What brought on the divorce? At first Lois did not connect it to her writing. Later, she began to see how the two were related. When she first married, she had be-lieved, or tried to convince herself, that running a house-hold was what she really wanted to do. But as the years wore on, she grew increasingly aware that she did not want to spend most of her time cooking, cleaning, and taking care of other people's needs.

As her children got older and needed less of her attention, she pursued her writing more. Her husband could not get used to this new person who was often away from home interviewing people, collecting information for her articles, doing what she wanted, and even earning money for it.

In middle-class American society in the 1950s and 1960s, most women were expected to stay home and take care of their families, while men were expected to have successful careers and earn the money to support their families.

A symbol of these common expectations for men and women existed in Lois's own house. Her husband, who always went to an office to work, nonetheless had a large study at home that was lined with books and dominated by an impressive desk. When Lois started to write, she did not claim a room of her own for her work. Instead, she set up a card table in a corner of her husband's study. That was her "office."

Seated at the card table, Lois wrote on a typewriter given to her by her father. One day she came home from a short business trip and walked into her husband's study. A glance at her card table revealed that the typewriter was not there. Upset, she immediately called her husband's office. "We've been robbed," she reported. "Somebody stole my typewriter."

"Relax," replied her husband. "No one stole your typewriter. I lent it to someone."

Lois was speechless. Her husband had lent her typewriter, the most important tool of her trade, without even asking her. It was a clear message to Lois that the man she had been married to for twenty-one years did not take her writing career seriously.

Lois, who had always wanted to be a writer, wanted her husband to be enthusiastic about her success when she began to realize her goal. She felt that Donald couldn't accept the changes in the way he pictured and thought of his wife. There was no room for Lois's career in their relationship. Divorce provided the only logical answer.

The couple's three oldest children were or would soon be on their own. Benjamin, the youngest, would stay with his father so he would not have to change schools to finish high school. Lois left the twelve-room house, the twenty-two acres of land, and the horses in the pasture and moved to a three-room apartment over a garage.

For the first time in her life, she was completely on her

own. Unable to support herself on the money she earned as a freelance magazine writer, she turned to photography to supplement her income. Her photos had begun to reflect her interest in children, so she decided to make a business of taking children's portraits. Years later, Lois remembered one of these portraits and used it on the cover of one of her books.

For two years after her divorce, Lois lived in Cape Porpoise, Maine, a small coastal town of some five hundred people, just up the road from fashionable Kennebunkport. When someone asked her to take photographs for a book called *Here in Kennebunkport,* she agreed, but it was strictly a business proposition, not a reflection of her own interests. What did interest her was writing novels for young people.

Although summers in Cape Porpoise were lovely, the Maine winters were brutal. Cold, damp winds blew through the small, oceanside community. The days were short and, when night fell, the streets were deserted.

Feeling isolated, Lois turned to movies, one of her greatest pleasures. However, the nearest theater was twenty miles away, and Lois's old car often wouldn't start in the cold. The second winter in Cape Porpoise convinced her that she needed to move to a place with lots of movies, lots of people, and lots of books. Boston seemed the perfect spot.

In 1979, Lois left Maine and rented a small, cozy apartment on Boston's fashionable Beacon Hill, an area of tidy brick rowhouses within walking distance of the Boston Common and other popular Boston attractions.

Because the apartment was too small for a darkroom, Lois could no longer make a living at photography. She was, however, writing novels at the rate of about one a year. Her high school yearbook prediction had come true. No longer a "future novelist," she was a novelist *now*.

Lois's mother,
Katharine Landis
Hammersberg

Lois's sister, Helen,
and Lois's mother,
July, 1935

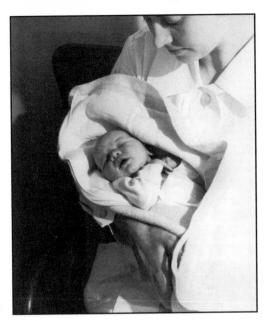

Lois Ann Hammersberg, 36 hours old

Helen, Lois, and their mother in 1937

*Helen and Lois
on Lois's
christening day,
February 20, 1938*

A curious Lois

Helen, Lois, and their mother at the 1940 World's Fair

Lois and Helen

Helen and Lois with their cousin

Lois, age 4

The young reader, 1941

*Lois and Helen
in 1941*

Lois's grandfather's home in Carlisle, Pennsylvania, setting for Autumn Street

Lois, age 8, in an uncharacteristically athletic pose

Lois in Tokyo, age 12

Lois's sixth-grade class in Carlisle, Pennsylvania.
Lois is third from the left in the front row.

Lois's high school
picture

Glogau

Lois Lowry on her wedding day, 1956

Lois with her husband and her father on her wedding day

Lois Lowry with her four children, 1964.
Clockwise from lower left: Alix, Grey, Benjamin, and Kristin.

*Clockwise from the top: Lois, grandson James,
daughter Alix, and daughter Kristin (James's mother)*

*Martin Small and
Lois with her son's
golden retriever*

Lois Lowry relaxing at home

*Annelise Platt,
Lois's friend from Denmark*

Bandit,
Lois's Tibetan terrier

Lois with Bandit

Lois and her granddaughter Nadine in November, 1994

Chapter 11
Books, Books, Books

"Where do you get your ideas?" readers often ask Lois Lowry. She admits it's a hard question to answer. Usually she replies, "Out of my imagination." Then she quickly adds that her imagination is fed by all the experiences she has ever had. That means, Lois says, "you must notice things if you want to write."

Lois Lowry has been noticing things all her life. Many of the things she has noticed have turned up in her books. Even books that seem to have nothing to do with her personal life contain bits and pieces of things she has observed over the years.

Her first book, *A Summer to Die*, came from her imagination and from reality—at least from her own interpretation of reality. In the novel, a family—mother, father, and two sisters—moves to a house in the country so that the father can finish a book he has been trying to write for a long time. The sisters, thirteen-year-old Meg and fifteen-year-old Molly, must now make friends in a new school. Meg, who believes Molly is prettier and more popular than she is, envies and dislikes her sister.

Meg becomes even more upset when Molly's frequent nosebleeds make her the center of their parents' attention and concern. When the family learns that Molly has incurable cancer, the crisis leads Meg to discover her own interests and talents, make her own friends, and accept herself and her sister as they are.

Clearly the plot of *A Summer to Die* grew out of Lois's experience of having a sister whom she envied and who died young. It is interesting that Lois chose this personal tragedy as the topic of her first novel. Perhaps the college professor who told her that experiencing grief might improve her writing had some influence on her after all.

If Lois had simply told the story of her sister's death, she would have been writing nonfiction, but she didn't want to do that. Instead, she wanted to shape her own experiences and feelings into a story that would be interesting to young people and give them something to think about. Although Lois and her sister Helen were in their twenties when Helen died, Lois changed the ages of the central characters. Young readers, she knew, wanted to read about people their own age. Lois combined how she felt about her sister when she was growing up with what happened when they were in their twenties. Other parts of the novel—the parents, the setting, the plot—came entirely from Lois's imagination.

When Lois's mother first read the book, she recognized the two sisters immediately. She also found in the book an incident that really happened between Lois and Helen. In the book, Molly draws a line down the center of the girls' shared bedroom to keep her younger sister's mess out of Molly's half of the room. According to Lois, Helen actually did the same thing once because she considered Lois such a slob. Lois also used another small detail from Helen's life, with a minor change. Recalling that Helen's high school sweetheart, Jack, gave Helen a silver football on a chain, Lois has Molly's boyfriend in *A Summer to Die* give Molly a silver basketball.

After writing a book that sprang from her own experience, Lois focused her second novel on a topic with which she had no experience at all—adoption. The book, *Find a Stranger, Say Good-bye*, tells the story of pretty, popular Natalie, whose life seems perfect. She has a warm, loving family, a congenial boyfriend, and good friends. She is about to graduate from high school and go to the college of her choice. The problem arises because Natalie, who knows she was adopted, wants to find out who and where her birth parents are. With her adoptive parents' reluctant consent, Natalie decides to spend the summer searching for her birth parents.

Although neither Lois nor any of her children were adopted, she believed this was an important story to tell. By law, most adopted children had been denied any information about their birth parents. At the time Lois wrote the book, the laws were changing. Lois knew the secrecy surrounding adoption troubled many young people, and she wanted to help them understand this issue. To get accurate facts so that she could create a realistic plot, she did research for her book. She talked to a judge, who explained the legal procedures for adoption in Maine, where the book takes place. She also spoke with adoptive parents and an adopted child to get a sense of their feelings about adoption.

However remote the topic was from her own life, Lois still found ways to bring her own experience into the book. She set the story in Maine, where she was living at the time. To portray accurately the lonely feelings of one character, she reached back to her own feelings of being an outsider when she returned to Carlisle as a ninth grader.

Find a Stranger, Say Good-bye was not universally praised when it first came out. Some book reviewers called it overly sentimental and thought the characters were too "nice." Other critics, however, found it well-written and satisfying. Because the topic was so timely and the plot of the book so interesting, the producers of television's Afterschool Specials made it into an hour-long TV movie.

For her third book, Lois went back to her own personal experience for inspiration. *Autumn Street* is her most autobiographical work and also her most troubling view of childhood. The novel takes place in a Pennsylvania town during World War II. The narrator, Elizabeth Jane Lorimer, is an adult when she tells the story of what happened when she was six years old. Elizabeth's father has gone off to fight in the war, and she has come with her mother and sister to live with a grandfather who loves her and a step-grandmother who does not like children at all. Shortly after Elizabeth's arrival, her baby brother is born. If all of this is beginning to sound familiar, read on.

As in Lois's real life, Elizabeth has three doting great-aunts, the sisters of her real grandmother. Lois added spice to real life by hinting that one of the sisters was also in love with Elizabeth's grandfather.

The novel even recalls the incident from Lois's childhood in which an escaped German prisoner stole clothes from a neighbor's clothesline. However, in the novel, Lois gave the situation more drama by having the narrator and her friend suspect the next-door neighbor's absent German husband of being a spy who was hiding in the attic.

Autumn Street is essentially the story of Elizabeth's friendship with Charles, the grandson of the family's black cook, and of Charles's murder. The cook, called Tatie in the book, is based on Fleta Jordan, who cooked for Lois's grandfather. Fleta Jordan had a granddaughter who was Lois's playmate and who was murdered long after Lois left Pennsylvania. Lois was surprised to learn that her step-grandmother had attended the funeral of Fleta Jordan's grandchild. Lois incorporated that event into *Autumn Street* because she felt it was a revealing act of humanity on the part of her step-grandmother, who had seemed so unsympathetic to Lois as a child.

Not surprisingly, Lois still describes *Autumn Street* as her favorite book. She has vivid memories of her childhood during the war years when she was living close to her mother's relatives in Carlisle, Pennsylvania. She enjoyed reliving those memories while writing the novel.

The book's somber theme made Lois feel that she needed to take an emotional break. As a lark, she wrote a short story about a ten-year-old free spirit named Anastasia Krupnik. Lois had the outspoken and imaginative Anastasia live in Cambridge, Massachusetts, with her father, a college professor, and her mother, a freelance artist.

Lois so enjoyed this character that she decided to expand the short story into a novel, and a few years later she expanded the novel into a series. So far, Lois has written nine books about Anastasia and two books about her precocious little brother Sam. The first book in the series, *Anastasia Krupnik,* was published in 1979, the same year that *Autumn Street* appeared and, as it happened, the same year that Lois Lowry moved from Maine to Massachusetts.

Was Anastasia based on someone Lois knew? Lois admits that Anastasia is probably a combination of her own two "quite nutty" daughters, who always thought for themselves and acted on their own decisions, sometimes to the dismay of Lois or their father.

Lois also says, however, that part of the inspiration for Anastasia was Amy Carter, the daughter of President Jimmy Carter, who was in the White House when the first Anastasia book was written. As Lois saw it, Amy Carter had a mind of her own and did what she wanted, seemingly unconcerned that millions of people might be reading about her escapades in the newspapers every night.

The plots of the Anastasia books came completely from Lois Lowry's imagination. Once again, however, Lois based incidents, details, and feelings on her own experiences. For example, in *Anastasia, Ask Your Analyst*, Anastasia suddenly finds herself embarrassed by her loving parents, whom, until very recently, she adored. Her folks assure her that it's just a stage she is going through. It's also a stage that Lois Lowry remembers vividly from her own adolescence. She recalls that until she was twelve, she thought her parents were "wise, wonderful, beautiful, and well-dressed." However, when she turned twelve and a half, almost overnight her parents became "stupid, boring people," and she didn't want to be seen in public with them. Clearly, at least a little piece of Anastasia comes directly from Lois's life.

Another incident from Lois's life turns up in *All About Sam*, the first book about Anastasia's little brother. When Sam enters his pet worm, King of Worms, in a pet show run by the local library, Anastasia tries to convince him that winning isn't important. Sam is not to be persuaded. He knows winning is important, and so do the judges, who award a prize to every entrant. Unfortunately, by the time the judges get to King of Worms, he has crawled out of his box. However, Sam still gets a prize—for the most invisible pet. Lois got this idea from a pet show run by the local library when her children were small. The judges actually did award a prize to every pet.

Will there be more Anastasia books? Probably. Lois intends to keep this heroine around as long as she finds her entertaining.

Although Anastasia has grown from ten to thirteen during the course of the series, she probably won't get any older. Lois is convinced that the readers who find a thirteen-year-old Anastasia captivating would not be interested in an older Anastasia.

After writing three Anastasia books and, in the second one, moving Anastasia and her family out of Cambridge and into the suburbs, Lois introduced a new heroine in *Taking Care of Terrific*. Enid Irene Crowley, a worldly fourteen-year-old, hates her name because it reminds her of all sorts of horrible words: horrid, putrid, squalid, stupid, sordid. Enid's family is a sharp contrast to Anastasia's. Enid's parents seem to have little time for their only child. In fact, the most stable presence in Enid's life is the live-in housekeeper, Mrs. Kolodny, who is given to such zany household blunders as confusing a box of instant mashed potatoes with a box of detergent, thus making the chowder inedible and the laundry unwearable.

Enid's life becomes more interesting when she takes a babysitting job. Her charge is four-year-old Joshua Warwick Cameron IV, better known to himself and Enid as Tom Terrific. Their escapades in the Boston Public Garden—culminating in an illegal midnight ride on the swan boats with a group of homeless women, a black college professor-musician, and a classmate of Enid's—change the lives of both Enid and Joshua by making them more aware of their connections to other human beings.

As Lois Lowry sees it, one of her goals as a writer for young people is to help her readers cope with the difficulties of being young in a world that doesn't always respect youth. In *Taking Care of Terrific*, the characters survive and, in a way, triumph, but their surroundings remain the same. It is still a world where some people are homeless and some children have parents who are more interested in themselves than in their children.

Lois's next book, *The One Hundredth Thing About Caroline*, also shows a realistic view of parents and children. Caroline and her older brother J.P. live in New York City with their mother, who barely makes ends meet on her salary as a bank clerk. The children's father has remarried, and Caroline and J.P. rarely see him. Despite the fact that the book addresses such topics as divorce and financial hardship, it is primarily a comedy. Caroline is just as wacky as Anastasia, but in her own unique way.

After reading a neighbor's discarded mail, Caroline becomes convinced that he is out to kill her and J.P. Of course he isn't, but it takes Caroline, her friend Stacy, and J.P. a while to figure this out. Their final enlightenment comes during a power outage in which their hilarious hijinks cause more problems than they solve.

Lois Lowry became so fond of Caroline and J.P. that she brought them back in two more books. In *Switcharound*, written in 1985, Caroline and J.P. go to Iowa—under protest—to spend the summer with their father, his second wife, and their three half-siblings. Given jobs they can't stand, Caroline and J.P. plot their separate revenges, until an unexpected turn of events at their father's sporting goods store helps them see their father and stepmother in a more sympathetic light. Then they must scramble to undo the truly creative revenges already under way.

The third book in the series was written in 1990. *Your Move, J.P.!*, brings them back to New York City and puts J.P. in the spotlight. When he falls hopelessly in love with a new girl at school, J.P. finds himself engaged in a mushrooming series of lies to impress her. He manages to figure out his true feelings while trying to win the chess championship during the school's annual Spring Fling, which he and his heartthrob attend dressed as—and in—golf bags.

As with the Anastasia books, Lois Lowry didn't plan to write a series when she wrote *The One Hundredth Thing About Caroline*, but the characters seemed to take on lives of their own. Lois regrets that the titles of the three books don't show they are about the same family, as the titles of the Anastasia and Sam books do. Readers who enjoy reading one book about Caroline and J.P. don't always know there are more in the series.

After writing *The One Hundredth Thing About Caroline* in 1983, Lois's next book tackled more serious issues. Like *Taking Care of Terrific, Us and Uncle Fraud* presents a view of adults as people who don't always live up to children's expectations. In this book, it is not the parents who don't measure up, but Uncle Claude, a free spirit who roams the world. When his money gets low or when he just doesn't know what to do next, Claude heads for his sister's house. Tom, Claude's older nephew, is already cynical about his uncle's unfulfilled promises, but the two younger children, Louise and Marcus, are enthralled when Claude tells them he has brought them a precious gift. However, when Uncle Claude disappears just after a wealthy home is robbed, they too become cynical. Then a raging flood threatens all three of the children. In the aftermath of the flood, the mystery of the robbery is solved, and Louise and Marcus discover what Uncle Claude's real gift to them is.

After amusing herself by writing two more Anastasia books and another Caroline and J.P. book, Lois again tackled a more serious topic in *Rabble Starkey*. Rabble is the nickname of Parable Ann Starkey, who has never known her father. Her mother, Sweet-Ho, was thirteen years old when she fell in love and ran off to get married. She was fourteen when Rabble was born. Now Rabble is twelve years old, and her father is long gone. Sweet-Ho supports the two of them by cleaning house for the Bigelow family and taking care of the two Bigelow children—Rabble's best friend Veronica and her sweet younger brother Gunther. When a depressed Mrs. Bigelow exhibits more and more bizarre behavior, she must go away to a hospital. Rabble and her mother move into the house so that Sweet-Ho can mother all three children. In their interactions with the neighborhood people, the children grow and change as they learn to cope with the situations that life hands them.

Rabble Starkey is one book for which Lois can pinpoint the source of her ideas. The novel started with a place and a topic. The place was southwestern Virginia, which she visits frequently because her brother and her father both live there. The area is quiet and rural, less crowded than New England. "Isolated in a good way," is how Lois describes it. Besides the beauty of the landscape, Lois likes the relaxed pace of life and the slow cadences of the natives' speech. In *Rabble Starkey*, she recreates both the speech patterns of the people and the area's leisurely life style.

The idea behind *Rabble Starkey* grew out of Lois's reading about teenage pregnancy. She thought about the phrase that people sometimes use to describe teen pregnancy, "babies having babies." Then she decided she wanted to tell a story from the point of view of someone who had been born to a very young mother. Once the setting and the topic were in place, the rest of the story about Rabble Starkey came easily.

After this serious book, Lois went back to the light-hearted Krupnik family. First she wrote *Anastasia's Chosen Career*. Then she added a new twist. Instead of focusing on Anastasia, she wrote *All About Sam*, in which Anastasia takes a back seat to her little brother Sam. When Sam got his own book, a series within a series was born.

After writing *All About Sam*, Lois tackled something she had never done before, a historical novel. This challenging and thought-provoking novel was to earn Lois universal praise—and her first Newbery Award.

Chapter 12
Newbery Books

Number the Stars takes place in Denmark during World War II, after Germany invaded and conquered that small nation. The novel tells the story of how one Danish family saved their Jewish friends from being rounded up and sent by the Nazis to a concentration camp.

Why did Lois choose this story to tell? Twenty-five years earlier, when she had first moved to Maine with her husband and children, she had met a Danish woman, Annelise Platt, the wife of one of her husband's law partners. Annelise and Lois became close friends, as did their children. Over the years, Annelise told Lois many stories of growing up in Denmark during World War II. Over and over again, Lois marveled at the Danish people's courage and determination to make sure that the Danish Jews did not go to Hitler's death camps.

Even after Lois moved to Boston, she and Annelise remained close friends. In the spring of 1988, they took a short vacation together to the island of Bermuda. Unfortunately for them, but fortunately for Lois's readers, the cold weather discouraged swimming. Also, Lois and Annelise did not have lots of money to spend in the expensive shops, so they sat and knitted and talked. As Lois often does, she pumped Annelise for stories about her childhood and about the time when the entire Danish population defied Hitler.

Among many other things, Annelise told Lois that during the war, the extreme cold and the shortage of heating fuel meant that children often wore mittens to bed to keep their hands warm. This small but vivid detail appealed to the writer in Lois. That's when she realized that big, historic events are made up of small details in the same way that all of her books are made up of small, vivid details.

Lois had always admired what the Danes had done. Now she felt ready to tell the story of their courage in her own way—from the point of view of two Danish children, one Jewish and one Christian, caught up in the horror of Hitler's mad attempt to exterminate Europe's Jews.

To tell this story, however, Lois needed more facts than Annelise could provide. So, for the first time since she began writing, Lois had to do extensive historical research. She spent part of the summer of 1988 in the stifling basement of the Boston Athenaeum, a private library, doing research on Denmark and World War II. Eventually, she completed her research and retreated to the relative coolness of her air-conditioned apartment to write the first draft of *Number the Stars*.

Just weeks before the manuscript was due, Lois decided that she wasn't satisfied with it. It needed something to bring it to life, and she knew what that something was. She had visited Denmark before, but she had to go there again to feel what it was like to stand where her characters would stand and to see what they would see.

Lois looked at her calendar. The trip seemed impossible. She had speaking engagements and other commitments right up to the time the manuscript was due. She looked more closely at the calendar. There were a few days between two of her commitments. Could she possibly squeeze a trip to Denmark into those few days? The travel agent was appalled. The airplane tickets would cost a small fortune unless Lois could book her ticket a month in advance of departure or stay in Denmark at least a week. But Lois could do neither of those things. She had to go when she had the time, and she had to stay for the few days she had available in her schedule, no matter what the cost. The book was worth it.

On the plane to Denmark, Lois chuckled when she looked at the itinerary she had made. While other tourists might make lists of museums and historic sites to visit, Lois had written down such things as "stand on the coast north of Copenhagen and smell the ocean." That was what she needed to do for her book, and that was what she did.

On her journey, Lois was fortunate to meet several people who had lived in Denmark during World War II. She met a woman who was a young bride in the early 1940s. The woman told Lois that *Gone with the Wind*, a romantic novel of the American Civil War, was popular reading at the time. Lois was surprised, but she wrote that detail into the book because it was real.

Also, near the end of her trip, Lois stood on the balcony of another Danish woman's apartment and listened to the woman describe the spontaneous celebration that broke out forty years before when the Danish people heard that the war was over. She told how people sang and danced in the square right below the balcony where Lois was standing. Lois used this information in her book, too.

After four busy days in Denmark, Lois returned home and rewrote *Number the Stars*. She didn't change the plot or the characters, but she did put Denmark into the book. The expensive and hectic trip proved to be well worth the cost and the effort, for when the book was published, it won the Newbery Medal for excellence in children's literature. According to librarians, it was the best children's book of 1989.

After the success of writing her first historical novel, Lois returned to some old friends: Anastasia and Sam, and Caroline and J.P. *Your Move, J.P.!* was published in 1990. *Anastasia at This Address* came out in 1991, and *Attaboy, Sam!* appeared in 1992.

Having had fun with some familiar characters, Lois

was ready to tackle another big challenge. Like *Number the Stars*, her next book would be different from anything she had written before. Whereas *Number the Stars* took her into the past, her new book, *The Giver*, would be a voyage into an imagined future.

In this future, all unpleasantness and pain have been removed from society, but along with these feelings have gone colors and passion and memory. Lois imagined that in this future, one person from each generation would be chosen to receive the society's collective memories, both good and bad. The person of the previous generation who held all these memories, The Giver, would pass them on to the next person to receive them. In the book, twelve-year-old Jonas is the chosen receiver.

As Jonas begins to experience both the pleasure and the pain denied everyone else, he also begins to question the very basis of his society. What happens to Jonas at the end of the novel Lois left open to interpretation. Many readers appreciate this opportunity to shape the book's meaning for themselves. A few would rather have answers, not questions. Most, however, agree that *The Giver* is Lois Lowry's most unusual book.

American librarians believed *The Giver* was an exceptionally powerful book. In 1994, they awarded Lois Lowry her second Newbery Medal in four years. When it came time for Lois to accept the Newbery Medal, she decided to try to answer the readers who were always asking, "Where do you get your ideas?"

Naturally, the plot and the characters for *The Giver* came entirely from her imagination. However, in her acceptance speech for the Newbery Award, she described some of the events in her life that led her to the themes and ideas she developed in *The Giver*. She pictured her memories as tributaries, all flowing into the river from which she drew inspiration for the book.

The first tributary she mentioned in her speech was the time she spent in Japan when she was twelve and thirteen years old. She was so curious then about the unfamiliar life around her, so eager to learn, yet restrained by a shyness that prevented her from reaching out to people.

Another tributary came from her college days, when she lived with a small group of women in a private house that had been converted into a dormitory. There was one girl who was "different," more quiet and studious than the others. The girls were not exactly cruel to her, but they ignored her and excluded her from their activities. Thinking back, Lois imagined what it would have been like to be this young woman who was set apart from the others.

Lois traced another tributary back to 1979, when she photographed and wrote about Carl Nelson, an artist living on an island off the coast of Maine. As they talked about color, Lois realized how important it was to this man. Years later she heard that Nelson had lost his sight.

Then, in 1989, Lois traveled to Germany for her son Grey's wedding to a German woman. A small part of the wedding ceremony was in English, a song based on words from the Old Testament. "Where you go, I will go. Your people will be my people." The song made Lois realize how small the world had become. She thought,

"We are all each other's people now."

Another tributary flowed into her river of ideas when Lois visited her father, who was almost ninety years old and lived in a nursing home. Family pictures hung on the walls of his room, and Lois and her father discussed the people in the photographs. One picture showed Helen. Looking at the photograph, her father said happily, "That's your sister. That's Helen." He didn't remember that she had died of cancer. Lois thought how comfortable it must be to forget such pain, but she wondered if forgetting the past was a safe thing to do. There were lessons to be learned from the past, and many good memories to go along with the painful ones.

Lois had been reminded of the lessons of history before, in 1991, when she spoke to a group of people about *Number the Stars*. Someone in the audience asked why people kept dwelling on the Holocaust, Hitler's attempt to exterminate the Jews. Why not just forget that unpleasant episode of history? After answering the question as best she could, Lois continued to think about it.

Perhaps people might feel more comfortable if they forgot the Holocaust, she thought, just as her parents felt safer and more secure sheltering her from life in Japan and insulating the family in the safe and familiar American village. For Lois, however, closing her life and her mind to different people and cultures and to painful memories did more damage than good. She remembered how she disobeyed her parents and went beyond the village to experience real life, to penetrate the wall that isolated people from each other. That, Lois thought, is why we remember the Holocaust, to be part of the whole of humanity and to understand so that we don't make the same mistakes over and over again.

Finally, Lois recalled in her Newbery acceptance speech a more recent memory. While sitting with her daughter in a restaurant, she had seen a television in the background and heard the newscaster announce that someone had walked into a restaurant and randomly killed several people. She held her breath, then sighed in relief. The killing had happened in a distant place. She had no need for concern. Then she realized her daughter was staring at her in disbelief. What difference did it make where the killing happened? It was still a tragedy. In that moment, Lois realized that she could not reduce her world to the neighborhood where she lived. Her world—everyone's world—is global, and the memories of that world—the painful ones as well as the happy ones—all count.

In her Newbery speech, Lois stated that all these tributaries of thought and experience came together in her mind to form the river of ideas that carried her through the creation of *The Giver*. In a sense, she gave a comprehensive answer to the question, "Where do you get your ideas?" The ideas behind the book, she explained, came from a host of past events and emotions.

In another sense, however, she didn't really answer the question. The plot, the setting, and the characters came from her extraordinary imagination, which cannot be explained, only appreciated.

Chapter 13
Occupation: Writer

Few people have the interest, the discipline, and the talent for a career as a writer. Lois Lowry has all three. What made her want to be a writer? Her shyness as a child certainly contributed to her interest in books and writing, as did the fact that her family moved many times during her youth. Lois was more comfortable with books than with the agonizing process of finding new friends among strangers, so she became an avid reader. It was a natural step from reading to putting her own story ideas into written words.

What made Lois Lowry write for young people? Her interest in remembering her own childhood is part of the answer. She likes to think about what her life was like and to transform that thinking into stories about fictional characters. In a way, she uses her writing to make sense of the frustrations, the fears, and the disappointments she has experienced.

Lois also writes for young people because so much of her early adulthood was spent observing and thinking about her own four children. She has said that when her children were teenagers, they put her through "every conceivable problem that one can have with adolescents." She learned from those experiences, and they made her realize how important it is to treat young people with sensitivity and compassion.

What makes Lois Lowry a good writer for young people is that she refuses to preach to them. Instead, her goal is to help her readers "answer their own questions about life." She realizes that today's teens have to be prepared to live in a complicated world. Through her writing, she wants to show them that they have choices in how they respond to the many situations they encounter.

That does not mean Lois takes herself too seriously. In fact, she has fondly described young people as "irreverent," an idea that allows her to give free rein to her own irreverent sense of humor.

How does Lois Lowry create a novel? The process differs depending on whether she is writing a series book or a single novel. When she adds another book to a series, she doesn't have to invent the characters or the setting.

Instead, she begins with the plot. What will happen? What conflict will arise? What problem will have to be solved?

If she is not writing for a series, she often starts with scattered ideas about characters and setting. For example, before sitting down to write one book, Lois thought about how much she liked the southwestern corner of Virginia, where her brother and father lived. At the same time, she saw many newspaper articles about teenage pregnancy. Those two ideas came together in her novel *Rabble Starkey*.

Being an enthusiastic gardener, Lois compares the process of starting a book to building a compost pile. When you build a compost pile, you toss in old leaves, grass cuttings, and vegetable matter from your garbage. After a while you have a nourishing mixture for growing plants. In the same way, when Lois writes, she tosses odd pieces of characters and settings into her mind and lets them mingle. After a while, without her even being aware of it, the odd bits and pieces come together into an idea for a book.

Once an idea lodges in Lois's mind, she begins to create in earnest. She imagines herself the age of the main character. One thing that helps her to do this is her extra-ordinary recall for what she felt like at different ages. For example, when she thinks about being twelve, she not only sees images, she also smells and tastes what it was like to be twelve.

If Lois doesn't have an image of a certain age from her own experience, she can always call on the information she has gathered from friends. She loves to question friends and acquaintances about their childhood memories. In fact, she has been known to quiz total strangers seated next to her on airplanes about their early years. Her emphasis is always on the small and the ordinary—the details that make her books seem so real to readers.

Sometimes this thinking stage is accompanied by research. *Number the Stars* required extensive library research about Denmark and its history during World War II. Lois also has done smaller research projects for other books.

When she was writing *The One Hundredth Thing About Caroline*, she made a whirlwind, one-day trip to New York City, the setting of the book, because she wanted to walk through the American Museum of Natural History, where Caroline, a budding paleontologist, liked to spend her time. To make sure the book was accurate, Lois needed a picture in her mind of where different exhibit halls were located in the museum and which ones Caroline would be likely to walk through.

This trip was especially fun for Lois because she went when her younger son, Benjamin, was visiting her during a college vacation. The two of them flew to New York in the morning, visited the museum, had lunch at a fancy restaurant, went to a play, had dinner at another fancy restaurant, and flew back to Boston the same night. It was a perfect blend of work and pleasure.

For most of her other books, Lois's research consists of drawing maps of the towns she has created and keeping track of information about the characters, such as their birthdays and their likes and dislikes, so that she doesn't write contradictory things in different parts of the same book. This is especially important in her two series, where what happens in later books must agree with what happened in earlier books.

Once the thinking stage and the research are completed, Lois sits down at her computer and starts to write. She has neither notes nor an outline. What she has are her characters, her setting, and usually a beginning and an ending in mind. The rest happens while she is sitting at the computer.

Lois is sometimes embarrassed to admit this is how she works, especially when she is talking to students and she knows their teacher wants her to say that it's important to outline or use note cards. Yet the process that works for Lois is thinking and creating, then writing spontaneously.

While Lois is writing a book, she revises the chapters as she goes. When she finishes the first chapter, she revises it. When she finishes the second chapter, she revises the first and the second, and so on. Lois has created this revision process because she doesn't work from an outline.

The writing stage of a book takes Lois a fairly short time compared to the thinking stage. Still, she writes every day. To get to her office, she descends a few steps from her tidy little kitchen into a glass-walled sun porch. From there, the steps reverse direction and go down into the finished basement of her house. A turn to the right and she is in a cozy office that is divided into two areas. One is a sitting area with a sofa, a wicker chest used as a table, and a chair. The other area is the work space. A computer desk sits against one wall and floor-to-ceiling bookcases line the opposite wall.

Here, unless she is traveling, Lois spends five hours a day writing. She is not always working on a novel, but she always has something to write. Sometimes she is asked to contribute to a book that will be a collection of stories or essays on the same topic but by different writers. Late in 1994, for example, she wrote an essay about Pennsylvania for a collection that featured essays about places by women writers.

Even if Lois isn't working on a writing project, she always has mail to answer. She gets piles of fan mail. In fact, since receiving her two Newbery Awards, she has gotten so much mail that she has had to hire a part-time secretary to help her answer the letters.

Of course, the most important writing is her novels. Sometimes, when she is working on a novel, she dreams that she has forgotten about a baby—forgotten to give it a name, forgotten to buy it clothes, even forgotten to feed it. When she finally does remember the baby, she discovers it is fine. It has a full set of teeth and it says, "Hey, I'm okay." Lois always has this dream when she feels she is neglecting a book she should be working on. The babies in Lois's dreams are the books she needs to write.

Occasionally, the ending of the dream is not happy. Lois drops the baby and it breaks. Sometimes, when the book or project she feels she has been neglecting is finished, she dreams that she puts the baby on a boat and waves good-bye.

In another dream about writing, Lois is living in a house—not one she has ever known—and suddenly discovers a door or a stairway leading to a series of enchanting rooms. The rooms are hard to get to, but they are so wonderful that they are worth the effort. Lois wakes from this dream feeling happy and realizing that the rooms are her books and other writing. She knows that, just like the rooms in her dream, her books are worth the effort it takes to create them.

When Lois is working on a novel, she doesn't talk to anyone about it or show it to anyone, not even Martin Small, her friend and companion for many years. Only once did she make an exception to this rule. When she finished her first draft of *The Giver*, she asked both Martin and her daughter Alix to read the manuscript because it was so different from anything she had written before. She wanted some feedback from those who were close to her.

Only when Lois has finished a book on her computer does she print it out. This, she always thinks, is her final copy. Of course, it never is. When she sends her manuscript to her editor, the editor reads it carefully and suggests changes, usually minor ones. For example, when her editor read *Us and Uncle Fraud*, he felt that the father was too harsh and that it was not clear enough that he cared deeply for his children.

Lois respects her editor's opinions and usually rewrites to accommodate the suggestions. In her second draft of *Us and Uncle Fraud*, for example, she softened the personality of the father. There was, however, one time when Lois couldn't bring herself to make a change that her editor wanted.

The book was *Number the Stars*, and the editor thought that Lois mentioned the shiny black boots of the Nazi officers too often. Lois didn't agree. Her friend Annelise Platt, who had been a child in Denmark during the war, had often mentioned the boots of the Nazi officers. Lois herself had noticed the boots when she had pored over old photographs from that period. She was also aware that the boots would be much more significant to a child than to an adult. Most children wouldn't dare look up into the face of an enemy soldier—they would instead focus on what children see best, the legs and feet.

A chance occurrence convinced Lois to stand by her feeling about the boots. In Australia on a book tour, Lois met a woman who was wearing a Star of David around her neck. It reminded Lois of the sketch she had seen for the book jacket of *Number the Stars* before she left Boston.

In conversation, Lois learned that the woman had been born in Holland to a Christian father and a Jewish mother. When the Nazis invaded Holland, both she and her mother were in danger of being taken to a concentration camp. Her parents tore up some planks in the floor of their home and made a space just big enough to hide a toddler. When the inevitable knock on the door came, they quickly put her under the floorboards.

Her mother was taken away that day, and the daughter never saw her again. When Lois asked the woman what she recalled about that day, the woman replied that because she was so young, her memories were not especially vivid, but the one thing she did recall was peeking out through a crack in the floorboards and seeing the high, shiny boots of the Nazi soldiers who came to take her mother away.

Lois returned to Boston and told her editor to leave in every single reference to the Nazis' high, shiny boots. After the book was published, while making a speech to accept the Newbery Award for the book, Lois told her audience, "I decided that if any reviewer should call attention to the overuse of that image—none ever has—I would simply tell them that those high, shiny boots had trampled on several million childhoods, and I was sorry I hadn't had several million more pages on which to mention that." [6]

Though most of the revisions Lois's editor has asked for are minor, one book went through extensive revisions. Just as Lois had asked Martin and her daughter to read *The Giver* before she sent it in, so her editor asked two other editors to read the manuscript at the same time he did. Each of the three editors sent Lois a list of questions the book had raised in their minds. They did not ask her to make specific changes in the manuscript, but they did ask her to consider the questions they raised.

Lois sat down with the three lists in front of her and revised the entire manuscript. For her, the revision was an exhilarating process. She was delighted to have the responses of three thoughtful readers to let her know where her book could be made clearer.

Once Lois makes the final revisions to a book on her computer, she prints out the manuscript and sends it off to the publishing company. Now her work is complete. Others take over. The book must be edited for grammar and punctuation, a typeface must be chosen, and the manuscript must be set in type. A book designer will decide what the cover should look like, and if the cover uses a drawing, an illustrator must be chosen.

Although many picture book writers create both words and illustrations for their books, it is unusual for a writer of novels to be involved in the illustrating. However, for two of her books—the Newbery Award winners—Lois provided the photographs for the book jackets.

For *Number the Stars*, the publisher asked Lois to write a more complete description of the main character so that the illustrator could be true to Lois's vision of her heroine. Instead of writing a description, Lois recalled a picture she had taken when she was photographing children for a living. She dug the photo out of her files. It was just what she thought Annemarie Johansen would look like. Ultimately, the photo was chosen for the cover of the book.

The cover of *The Giver* also features a photograph taken by Lois years earlier when she interviewed and photographed Carl Nelson, the artist who lived on an island off the coast of Maine. When she finished writing *The Giver*, Lois felt that photograph was the perfect representation of the character of The Giver.

Once a book has been written, edited, designed, and set in type, it is ready to go to the printer, and from there to bookstores. Lois's work is done, and it is now time to wait for the reactions of readers and reviewers. From the beginning, most reviewers have applauded both the style and content of her books. However, some have found fault with certain aspects of particular books. Lois is always interested in these critical comments, but she has never been devastated by them. She says that for a review to really crush her, the reviewer would have to notice some flaw in the book that Lois knew about and was hoping no one else would see. So far that has never happened.

Lois doesn't mind criticism of her books, but she doesn't pay much attention to a negative review if she feels that the reviewer has not read the book carefully. That was the case with a review of *The Giver*. The reviewer criticized the book for being racist because the main characters were all white and for being sexist because the job of taking care of The Giver in his old age fell to a woman, his daughter. Neither of these criticisms was based on the facts of the book, so Lois felt justified in ignoring that review.

Readers also let Lois know what they think of her books. *The Giver* has brought Lois an enormous amount of mail, probably because its ending is left to the reader's interpretation. Many have written to tell Lois how much they appreciated this and to share with her what their interpretations were. Some, however, were not happy with having to provide their own interpretations. One boy wrote Lois to tell her that the ending of *The Giver* was "a bummer."

What can readers expect from Lois Lowry in the future? Lois has said that she will keep writing Anastasia books until she tires of Anastasia. She will also continue to stretch her creative talent as she did with *Number the Stars* and *The Giver*.

After winning the Newbery for *Number the Stars*, she was asked whether the honor made it harder to write her next book because she might be afraid that she wouldn't be able to live up to people's new expectations. On the contrary, Lois replied, winning the Newbery had actually freed her to take risks. Having won the highest award she could, she was no longer concerned with anyone else's judgment of her work. The result was *The Giver*, the most unusual book she has written so far, and another award winner.

Does Lois want to try new audiences, perhaps adults or younger children? Actually, she has already written a few picture books for younger children, but none of them have been published. Her editor prefers that she stick to one audience, readers between the ages of eight and sixteen who eagerly await each new novel. Still, every once in a while she gets an urge to write a picture book, and she sends it off to her editor. Sometimes the editor says reluctantly, "Do you want me to try to find an illustrator for this?" So far Lois has said no.

Sometimes people ask Lois if she has considered writing for adults. This question annoys her, especially if the person asking implies that writing for adults is more important than writing for young people. Lois feels that what she is doing is important work, just as important as writing for adults. She also feels that the only real difference between books written for adults and books written for young people is the age of the main character.

Without actually writing *for* adults, Lois is finding that her books are being enjoyed *by* adults. This is especially true of *The Giver*, which has appeared on a number of reading lists that suggest titles for informal book discussion groups. Also, many young people are reading *The Giver* and then asking their parents to read it so they can talk about it together.

What about retirement? Will Lois Lowry ever stop writing? For now, the answer is "No plans for retirement." And why should she retire? Lois is doing what she loves, and doing it well. What more could she or her readers ask?

Her editor certainly doesn't expect her to stop. He called her Newbery Award-winning book *The Giver* an exceptional book, but he also said that he thought Lois Lowry's best book was yet to come. All her readers have to do is wait.

Chapter 14
In Her Spare Time

Even a dedicated and busy writer like Lois Lowry doesn't spend all of her time writing. She has varied interests and many activities. First among them is keeping in touch with her family.

Her younger son, Benjamin, lives closest to her in a Massachusetts coastal town north of Boston. From there he commutes north to Portland, Maine, to practice law with his father.

Lois's younger daughter, Kristin, lives in Maine with her twelve-year-old son, James, Lois's first grandchild. Lois enjoys being a grandparent, and her relationship with her grandson is much more relaxed and informal than the one she had with her own grandparents.

On one of Lois's visits, when James was six years old, his mother had given him the task of learning one new word every day. On that particular day, the word was *drama*. To help James understand the word, his dramatic grandmother began energetically acting out the story of "Little Red Riding Hood," playing all the parts herself. Kristin suggested that if James didn't like his grand–mother's performance, it was an old custom to throw rotten tomatoes at unsatisfactory players. James immediately disappeared into the garden to look for rotten tomatoes. To his grandmother's relief, James found no tomatoes that day. But if there had been, no doubt Lois would have been a cheerful target, all in the interest of a language lesson, of course.

Lois's older son, Grey, was in the United States Air Force and had been stationed in Germany for some time. In 1989, he married a German woman named Margret. Four years later, Margret gave birth to Lois's second grandchild, a girl named Nadine. At Thanksgiving in 1994, Lois traveled to Germany to see her granddaughter for the second time. Sadly, Grey died in an airplane crash in May of 1995 while on duty in Germany.

Lois's oldest child, Alix, became a computer specialist and, for a long time, lived in Boston. She and Lois saw each other frequently. Alix now lives in San Francisco.

Another very special person came into Lois's life in 1979. That was when she met Martin Small. He is also divorced and, between them, he and Lois have eight grown children. On the rare occasions when the extended clan gathers, Lois and Martin's small home overflows.

For many years, Lois and Martin lived in an apartment in Boston's Beacon Hill area, not far from the gold-domed Massachusetts State House, the Boston Public Garden where the swan boats glide, and the company that has published all of Lois's novels. Because the Beacon Hill apartment was so small, Lois rented another small space as an office and went there every day to write.

In 1983, Lois and Martin bought an old farmhouse in rural New Hampshire, a few hours drive from Boston. There they retreat on weekends for rest and recreation and a taste of country life. Remarkably, even though they bought the farmhouse six years after the publication of Lois's first novel, *A Summer to Die*, it closely resembles the house she described in that novel.

In spring and summer Lois enjoys gardening at her country retreat. Gardening is a favorite hobby that she doesn't have space for in the city. In front of the windows at the New Hampshire house, Lois has planted clusters of yellow helenium, Helen's flower, in memory of her sister.

In 1993, Lois and Martin decided it was time to leave their cozy Beacon Hill apartment. Martin was about to retire. He and Lois felt that if they were both going to be at home most of the time, they needed more space. Besides, Lois had wanted a dog for a long time, and the owners of the apartment building did not allow pets.

They went house-hunting in Cambridge, a city just across the river from Boston. Eventually they found their new home—a small, square, two-story brick house. It is just the right size for them and for Bandit, the Tibetan terrier that joined their household after the move. Bandit gets his name from the fact that if you lift all the fur that normally falls over his eyes, you can see two dark eye patches that look like a bandit's mask.

Whether at home in Cambridge or in New Hampshire, Lois finds pleasure in a few quiet activities. She is rarely without a knitting project or a book to read. Just as young people enjoy reading about characters close to their own age, Lois likes reading books by and about women, especially middle-aged women like herself. She also enjoys biographies and personal memoirs, books written by people who are sifting through events of their lives and reflecting upon them, just as Lois does when she writes a novel.

What she does not read, at least not very often, is books by other writers for young people, except for books sent to her by authors who are her friends. These she reads and enjoys.

Among Lois's friends who write for young people is Paula Danziger. "Yes," she laughs, realizing the inevitable question of her readers, "I do know Judy Blume. I've been to her house."

When she isn't knitting, reading, or getting together with family and friends, Lois is likely to watch a movie. She loves movies, and if she isn't going out to a theater to see a new film, she likes to create her own film festivals by renting movies from the local video store. For example, she will rent only Australian films for a week, or she will go through a period of watching only films by her favorite screenwriter, Horton Foote (who wrote the screenplay for *To Kill a Mockingbird*).

Lois once said that the one thing she wished she had done in her life was study filmmaking. A friend, the writer Bruce Brooks, heard this remark and asked Lois what she thought she would enjoy about filmmaking. She answered that if she were involved in filmmaking, she would want to write the script, design the sets, be in charge of the cinematography (the visual look of the movie), and direct the movie. Bruce replied that she sounded like someone who should write books.

Immediately Lois saw his point. As the author of a book, she writes the dialogue, designs the settings, vividly portrays scenes, and controls the overall direction of the book. Besides that, she does the casting, the costume design, and a host of other jobs that have to be divided up among many workers on a movie. Since that conversation, Lois has felt no regrets about not studying filmmaking.

Besides, a close encounter with filmmaking taught Lois firsthand some of the difficulties and disappointments of translating a written work into a visual medium. In 1980, Lois adapted her second novel, *Find a Stranger, Say Good-bye,* into a screenplay for an Afterschool Special entitled "I Don't Know Who I Am." The TV special was well- received and even nominated for an Emmy Award. However, Lois was disappointed because the film didn't look the way she had visualized her story. For one thing, the novel takes place in Maine, but the Afterschool Special had to be filmed in California because it was less expensive to make it there. Although this didn't interfere with the plot or characters, the setting looked different from the way Lois had pictured it. To avoid future disappointments of this sort, she has steadfastly refused offers to turn her Anastasia books into a TV series.

Compared to movies, sports play a relatively small part in Lois's leisure time. Only one spectator sport gets her attention—professional football. She's an enthusiastic though not particularly loyal fan, blithely switching her allegiance depending on how various teams are doing. In 1994, she was a vocal supporter of her home team, the New England Patriots. After a slow start they had a great year, at least until the playoffs, when they lost to the Cleveland Browns. However, in 1981, when the Oakland Raiders won the Super Bowl, they were her favorite team, and her favorite player was Raider Marcus Allen. In fact, she liked him so much that she later named a character after him in her book *Us and Uncle Fraud*.

Since childhood, Lois has avoided participating in most sports. She is comfortable now admitting that she felt she never had the coordination and timing to be a good athlete. For years she did brave the snowy slopes for downhill skiing, perhaps because of her Nordic heritage. A few years ago, she gave that up and now limits herself to cross-country skiing. Recently a guest at her New Hampshire country home laid some cross-country ski trails, so now Lois can ski from her back door.

Lois got an early start as a traveler, sailing from Hawaii to New York City at the age of two, and she has continued to travel throughout her life—both for business and pleasure. As a writer for young people, she is invited to speak at numerous conferences all over the country. Sometimes these conferences are in places that she also wants to visit.

One of her most memorable trips took place in 1982 when she spoke at a conference in Pennsylvania. After her speaking duties were over, she made a trip to Carlisle and took a nostalgic walk through the town, remembering the experiences of her childhood.

The favorite haunt of her youth, the public library, was still there, but it seemed smaller than she remembered. Lois quickly bounded up the front staircase, recalling how high and steep it had seemed when, as a small child, she had trudged up the steps burdened with the many books she had to return.

Her grandfather's house still stood, but it was now a part of the college and closed for the summer. She wondered if books still lined the walls of the room that had been the library and if, where the dining room had been, there was still a small buzzer under the rug that her grandmother had pressed with her foot to call the maid.

As Lois wandered around Carlisle, she recalled some ghosts of the past: a fourth-grade bully named Gene and a drooling, bad-tempered Saint Bernard that she tried to avoid on her many trips to the library.

Amid all the ghosts, however, there was one living person in Carlisle who still remembered her. Fleta Jordan, who used to cook for her grandparents, was ninety-five years old and dying of cancer. The last time Lois had seen her was twenty years earlier at Helen's funeral.

Lois went to visit Fleta in her small house near the railroad station. Lois had never been there before, because in the 1940s it would have been unthinkable to visit a black servant in her home. Lois brought Fleta a copy of *Autumn Street*, the book in which she memorialized her childhood. Fleta is in the book as the character called Tatie. During her visit, Lois asked about the many pictures of Fleta's family displayed around the house. One showed a young woman, a grandchild, in a cap and gown at her college graduation. Fleta told Lois that the woman's name was Lois, too, and that she had been named for her.

The trip to Carlisle was a journey back in time. Other travels have taken Lois around the world. Several years ago, her publisher sent her on a book-signing tour to Australia and New Zealand. It is typical of Lois that on this trip she made connections with people in surprising ways. Before she left the United States, she received a note from an Australian writer. The woman said she admired Lois's work and wished she could meet Lois but probably wouldn't because she lived far from where Lois was scheduled to stop. In any case, she wanted to welcome Lois to Australia.

Lois arrived in Australia and began her schedule of bookstore visits and talks. At one bookstore, she was at the point in her talk when she chose someone in the audience to receive one of the Boston T-shirts she had brought along with her. Usually she did this by having an

Anastasia look-alike contest. This often meant picking out a young girl who wore glasses. However, at this gathering there were no bespectacled girls, so Lois decided on a new scheme. She had read that in any group of fifty people, two of them would be likely to have the same birthday. So she said she would give the T-shirt to anyone who shared her birthday. She teased the audience about the date for a bit, finally revealing that the month was March. Then she began a countdown to the day. When she finally admitted that the date was March 20, a woman near the back of the room spoke up. March 20 was her birthday, too. Surprisingly, she was the same author who had written to Lois in the States.

Lois has also made many trips with Martin—to Norway, where she visited her ancestral village of Hammersberg (now part of Oslo), to Hawaii and Fiji, to the Swiss Alps, and to the Serengeti plain of Africa. It was there in the early 1980s that Lois and Martin had their one unpleasant travel experience. They were in a Nairobi park by themselves when a group of local people started asking them questions about the United States. Martin and Lois were so eager to share information with these people that they didn't notice they were being maneuvered to a quiet area of the park where there were no other tourists. When they were a safe distance away from anyone else, the people who had been quizzing them took all of Lois's and Martin's money. Lois and Martin were unharmed but embarrassed at having fallen so easily into a trap.

In the winter of 1994, Lois and Martin made perhaps their most unusual trip, a cruise to Antarctica. The trip was Lois's retirement present to Martin and also a measure of her affection for him since she hates the cold and doesn't particularly like being on boats, both of which Martin loves. On top of that, shortly before the trip, Lois fell down a flight of stairs and spent the entire trip with her foot in a cast. Although this trip was not one Lois would have chosen for herself, she did find things to enjoy. Antarctica provided some spectacular scenery that Lois took pleasure in photographing.

Shortly after the Antarctica trip, Lois and Martin took a vacation in which the situation was reversed. She loved it; he didn't. In the spring of 1994, they spent eight days rafting down the Colorado River and through the Grand Canyon with a group of twenty or so other people. Lois was surprised that she enjoyed the trip. Not an experienced camper, she had never thought of herself as the "outdoorsy" sort. Yet, for her, seeing the staggering beauty of the landscape and being in a place so remote from civilization more than made up for the lack of physical comfort.

In the summer of 1994, Lois made another trip—this time with a new traveling companion. Years before, she had promised her grandson James that when he turned eleven, they would take a trip together. James chose Hawaii as the destination. He and Lois spent nine days there, mostly swimming and enjoying the beaches. At night, they went back to the hotel after dinner to watch a rented movie. Since this vacation was Lois's treat to her grandson, she cheerfully sat through three screenings of *Ace Ventura, Pet Detective* in nine days.

Lois also plans to return to Japan, possibly visiting the Meguro School where she attended seventh and eighth grade. Mainly she wants to travel to the remote areas of Japan where people are few and the scenery is superb.

Japan will be another homecoming for Lois Lowry, as was her trip to Carlisle in 1982 and her trip to Hawaii in 1994. She has had many homes throughout the years and, wherever she has lived, she has been a keen observer of the life around her. Everything she has seen and experienced has contributed to making her the person and the writer she is today.

Who is Lois Lowry today? She is a woman who knows what she wants and does it. She is a writer who is both very serious and laugh-out-loud funny. She is someone who cares deeply about young people. In her own words, she is someone who is happy.

Many years ago, in her first book, Lois had one of her characters say, "I like to think that someday, when I'm grown up, people everywhere will know who I am, because I will have accomplished something important— I don't even know yet what I want it to be, just that it will be something that makes people say my name . . . with respect." [7]

People say Lois Lowry's name with respect, with affection, and with anticipation. What will she write next?

Notes

1 Adele Sarkissian, ed. *Something About the Author Autobiography Series, Volume 3*, Detroit: Gale Research Company, 1987, p. 136.

2 *Ibid.*

3 *Ibid.*

4 *Ibid.*

5 Lois Lowry, "Crow Call," *Redbook*, December, 1975, vol. 146, pp. 38-39.

6 Lois Lowry, Newbery Medal Acceptance Speech, *Horn Book*, July/August, 1990 (vol. 66).

7 Lois Lowry, *A Summer to Die*, Boston: Houghton Mifflin, 1977.

Time Line

1937   Lois Ann Hammersberg is born on March 20 in Honolulu, Hawaii

1939   Family moves to Brooklyn, New York

1942   Father goes off to war; Lois, her sister, and their mother move to Carlisle, Pennsylvania

1948   Family moves to Japan

1950   Lois, her mother, and her siblings move back to Carlisle

1951   Family moves to Governors Island, New York City

1954   Lois graduates from Packer Collegiate Institute and enters Pembroke College of Brown University

1956   Lois leaves Pembroke and marries Donald Grey Lowry

1958   First child, daughter Alix, is born

1959   Second child, son Grey, is born

1961   Third child, daughter Kristin, is born

1962   Fourth child, son Benjamin, is born; sister, Helen, dies

1963 Lois and family settle in Maine

1972 Lois receives her B.A. from the University of Southern Maine

1977 Lois's first novel is published; Lois is divorced

1979 Lois moves to Boston

1990 Lois wins the Newbery Medal for *Number the Stars*

1994 Lois wins the Newbery Medal for *The Giver*

Novels by Lois Lowry

A Summer to Die, 1977

Find a Stranger, Say Good-bye, 1978

Autumn Street, 1979

Anastasia Krupnik, 1979

Anastasia Again!, 1981

Anastasia at Your Service, 1982

Taking Care of Terrific, 1983

The One Hundredth Thing About Caroline, 1983

Anastasia, Ask Your Analyst, 1984

Us and Uncle Fraud, 1984

Anastasia on Her Own, 1985

Switcharound, 1985

Anastasia Has the Answers, 1986

Rabble Starkey, 1987

Anastasia's Chosen Career, 1987

All About Sam, 1988

Number the Stars, 1989

Your Move, J.P.! 1990

Anastasia at This Address, 1991

Attaboy, Sam! 1992

The Giver, 1993

Anastasia Absolutely, 1995

About the Author

Since graduating from Middlebury College in Vermont in 1966, Lois Markham has been an English teacher, an editor, and a writer. She has written biographies of Theodore Roosevelt, Thomas Edison, and Helen Keller. She is also a frequent contributor to *Kids Discover* and has written issues of the magazine on the five senses, bubbles, Columbus, Colonial America, the rain forest, rivers, and energy.

In her spare time, Lois enjoys reading, acting in amateur theatricals, tap dancing, and walking in the woods or along the beach. She loves being a mother, leading a Brownie troop, and volunteering in the library at her daughter's school.

Lois lives in Beverly, Massachusetts, with her husband and their eight-year-old daughter, Amy.

Index